One Last Summer

One Last Summer

Dick Sullivan

A Coracle Book

By the same author:

Non-fiction
Navvyman
The Nature of Things: Plato Now and Then

Fiction
Gideon's God

Poetry
Hills of Age

ISBN: 978-0-906280-13-3

For Mary

Contents

Preface   ix

Part 1 – Platonism Today

Chapter I   Platonism in Brief   3

Chapter II   Undertones of Eternity   7

Chapter III   Culture and the Expanded Mind   13

Chapter IV   Christianity   17

Chapter V   Limits and the Unlimited   21

Chapter VI   Last Things   25

Part 2 – Aspects of Platonism

Chapter I   Wordsworth: The Poet
                and the Contracted Mind   31

Chapter II   De Profundis   39

Chapter III   Old Man in a Dry Month   43

Chapter IV   The Scholar-Gipsy   55

Chapter V   Plays and Platonism   63

Chapter VI   Poetry and Platonism   67

Chapter VII   Plato in Pictures   79

Chapter VIII   Music's Magic Casement   89

Chapter IX   Plato, Ruskin and the Welfare State   95

Chapter X   Ruskin the Platonist   103

Part 3 – Decline and Fall

Chapter I   Wordsworth Platonised   113

Chapter II   The De-Platonising
                of William Wordsworth   125

Chapter III   Coleridge: "A Hunger for Eternity"   139

Chapter IV   Inventing Oblong Wheels   143

Chapter V   An Abuse of Reason   153

Chapter VI   The Arts: "A Kind of Anxiety"   163

Chapter VII   Forgetting Obvious Things   169

Part 4 – One Last Summer

Chapter I   Summary   175

Chapter II   Last Word   179

Notes and Additions   183

Index   221

Preface

So have I heard the cuckoo's parting cry,
From the wet field, through the vext garden-trees,
Come with the volleying rain and tossing breeze:
The bloom is gone, and with the bloom go I!

MATTHEW ARNOLD

The "last summer" of the title was meant to be that of 2020, the year of plague and panic. The plan was to stay a while in some of England's more rural places to note and record those undertones of eternity which run throughout this book. Serial lockdowns ended that and, since a year when you're already old can age you rapidly, that part of *One Last Summer* will never now get done. I used the year to cannibalise earlier books - *Undertones, Counter-Cosmos, Aphrodite Rising* - into a more coherent account of Platonism, often highly condensed and a bit piecemeal and patchwork.

Today a Platonist has to be self-taught because there are no teachers. My self-education began just before dawn on 1st January 2008. I'd be seventy in a few weeks but with nothing really achieved, not a life well-lived. I could reasonably bank on another five years but what to do to make amends? For many years I'd made my living writing film scripts and commentaries and had written a book or two, and so writing it had to be. But what theme? My only idea was based on a recurring experience which had begun nearly seventy years earlier …

…in 1942 in Mardale in Westmorland where the Haweswater dam was already almost finished. Manchester Corporation had built a village of huts on the fellside at Burnbanks but school for navvy children was in Bampton a couple of miles down the lane. Wartime schooling began at four years old and, come snow or shine, we walked those few miles to and fro each day. One morning in the Spring of 1942 we were taken on a "nature ramble" on the fells above the school. Up there in the first warm sunshine of the year I came upon a hedge, with the briars of a bramble bush stark against a blue sky, overlooking the Lowther valley. There came a dissolving through that green landscape into a Beyond which was home. It took another seventy years before I realised that what I experienced that day was not only eternity but more specifically a Platonic eternity.

One Last Summer has three themes: sensing eternity through beauty: the rightness of a mind illuminated by learning: what happens when both are lost. Beauty connects us to eternity. Ugliness - in ideologies, ideas, broken landscapes and ruined psychologies - is actively destructive. The West has forgotten obvious things, and the absence of a spiritual core has left a void filled with self-pity, resentment and rage.

An asterisk (*) indicates there's an entry in the Notes and Additions section.

Dick Sullivan

PART ONE

—

Platonism Today

CHAPTER I

Platonism in Brief

Our home is a far country and beauty takes us there.

Like amphibians, we live in two worlds – in our case, the material and the spiritual. Both must be in balance. If one decays, the other can't flourish and will also fade away.

When the free current of the religious life is dammed up … it turns into a swamp, and poisons human society.

We cannot make a religion for others, and we ought not to let others make a religion for us. Our own religion is what life has taught us. If we can clarify this body of experience, which comes to us so turbid and impure, we shall have done what is best worth doing for ourselves … and we shall have to offer to others the best that was in us to give.

When I speak of the Platonic tradition, I mean the actual historical development of the school of Plato. It is no part of my subject to discuss whether the school rightly interpreted their master.

Platonism is a genuine faith, a living interpretation of life, by which men have guided their conduct and moulded their thoughts.

DEAN INGE*

Our home is eternity and beauty takes us there.

Eternity is the peace which tells us all will be well*.

Undertones of eternity are experienced through the beauty
of the world, the daily miracle of common things.

Undertones are always coupled with a sense of sadness for
the loneliness of things, the melancholy of exile.

Platonism is also the way of the intellect, of mind illuminated by the right kind of learning, and the equally vital
examined life.

The arts should expand the mind, deliver beauty and generate undertones.

Ugliness - in flawed ideologies and cultures, in damaged
psychologies, vandalised landscapes and stunted lives - is
destructive.

The loss of beauty and the eternal can end in an abyss easily
colonisable by rage and resentment, self-pity, malevolence
and despair.

Christianity can add to Platonism since its theology is less esoteric, more earthy and life-centred.

The immaterial is more important than the material.

Platonism is immaterialist - the immaterial (eternity) is primary and all else is held in it.

The soul is what senses eternity and so is itself eternal.

CHAPTER II

Undertones of Eternity

Beauty is the sign of another and higher order.

ROGER SCRUTON

Beauty is but the sensible image of the Infinite.

LORD VERULAM

These fragments I have shored against my ruins.

T S ELIOT

There are two ways to reach that sense of eternity - inner (introvertive) and outer (extrovertive)*. Both happen when the mind stops thinking and eternity floods in to fill the void. The first is via painstaking meditation, conscious mind stilling often with the help of mantras and other tricks. The second is spontaneously gifted through the beauty of the world. But these extrovertive experiences also lie along a spectrum from greater to lesser. Undertones are the lesser kind, minor, elusive, fleeting, ungraspable, inexplicable, like peripheral sight. Wordsworth, I suspect, was subject to the major ones while

7

lesser poets such as John Masefield* experienced what he called "fragments".

Generally, undertones are evoked by smaller but always beautiful things: light and shadows on a wall, old weathered dressed and sculpted stone, rain, ruins, landscape, blue hills, church bells, greenery, colour, impressions in paint, summer, rhyme. The lime avenue leading to a conclusion, a passage to a place. Summer is the Platonist season, summer in a lane in sultry weather with the flowers still in bloom, leaves silent and drooping in the heat: the deep lonely calm of summer in an intensity of green. Birdsong - in the city the blackbird sings in the Spring: in deep country the cuckoo calls through the heat of summer when life is fulfilled in all its fecundity and stillness, closer to eternity. Then there's the melancholy of those long twilights: a day is nearly done like life itself but with the hope of a resurrection, another fine day.

Beauty is in water over a fall, or weir. Wind in the trees - a half gale in a midnight country lane with scudding cloud and the roar of tossing boughs. Windows - but only when alone in an empty room, standing back, treating them as frames for a garden or gated wall. A wooden staircase rising and turning. We find beauty in poetry/art, the illumination of learning, a wholeness of life, in belonging to a place and in continuity through time.

There's no evidence that Dorothy Wordsworth shared her brother's vision, in fact the opposite, but she was alive to the causes of undertones and noted them down in the journal which she began in Alfoxden in the great year of 1798. Many of the notes are homely (going to the shoemaker's, a trip to a farm for eggs, starching linen) but with sharp observations: from the summit of the Quantocks the sound of the sea is lost in "the noiseless noise" of summer: locks of wool spangled with dew: sheep glittering in the sun: a rainbow coloured halo round the moon: a lane glinting like a river: trees that almost roared in a storm: girls in the hills in their summer dresses and pink and blue petticoats: honeysuckle budding, hazels in blossom: flies spinning in the sun: the mountains of Wales islanded in sunshine: the night cloudy but not dark (a line which reappears in Coleridge's *Cristabel*).

Poetry should also lodge Masefieldian fragments in the mind: you may forget the details of *The Odyssey* but the imagery, the undertones stay in the mind for a lifetime: Calypso and Circe, Cyclops tall as trees. Prose can do the same: you may not remember who said what in *Alice in Wonderland* or may have been dismayed by the shallowness of the plots in Sherlock Holmes but the undertones of Carroll's strange world and Conan Doyle's Victorian London will be always be there.

A feeling of sadness and stillness is a strange secondary aspect of undertones. English has no word single word for it, suggesting it's never been singled out as important. Instead there are only phrases: *lacrimae rerum* or *tears for things* and perhaps Aristotle's *golden melancholy*. The Japanese, I believe, have a deeper understanding of all this - at least, their language seems to have four words for four moods: s*abi, aware, jugen, wabi. Sabi* is sadness for the loneliness of things, *aware* for their fading away, for their passingness, *jugen* for the oddity of here. *Wabi,* less Platonically, is a sense of greaterness, more awe perhaps than sadness. To experience these things you need *miyabi* (sensitivity to delicate degrees of beauty) and *fuga* (sensitivity to the four moods) - or at least so R H Blyth* tells us.

John Ruskin (1819-1900) was the first, I believe, to isolate this mood in the West: he called it "sadness and repose" and it suffuses all great art. Why is this? Perhaps because stillness, like beauty, is an attribute of eternity and so reconnects us. Sadness is natural to a species dislodged from its home, aliens exiled from eternity. It's also an undertone-like experience, a mingling of melancholy and peace. The main mood is the loneliness of things, followed by their fleetingness.

Auden coined the word "topophilia" to describe the way John Betjeman felt about landscapes rooted in time. It means love of a place which human hands have shaped over the centuries. Deep Time, too, can be an undertone, a connector to non-time or the eternal. Jacquetta Hawkes advises you to look at your hand and "feel its bones and nails" and then try to visualise "dark, warm mud squeezing between scaly claws". Her book, *A Land*, written in the 1940s when she was in her own thirties, is about the living presence of the deep past in the present. In it she traces the history of England from the laying down of the rocks to the coming of people and what they did to the landscape. It's also a mysticism of place and its poetry. "Hardy's poems grew from the Wessex downlands, Clare's from the tiny stretch of the Midlands in which alone he felt at home; Crabbe's are the bitter fruit of the Norfolk (sic) Coast:

> There poppies, nodding mock the hope of toil,
> There the blue bugloss paints the sterile soil.

Goldsmith's *The Deserted Village* and Gray's *Elegy* are better, redolent of the 18th century but filled with undertones of an eternity alien to that age of reason:

> Now fades the glimmering landscape on the sight,
> And all the air a solemn stillness holds,
> Save where the beetle wheels his droning flight,
> And drowsy tinklings lull the distant folds.

Children's books are particularly good at creating fragments. Boys who read (or read in the past) *Treasure Island* also take in lifelong undertones revolving around Long John Silver, Blind Pew, Billy Bones, Captain Flint dying in Savannah calling for rum, and Ben Gunn craving a little bit of toasted Christian cheese - not that he said that exactly, of course, no more than Holmes said "elementary, my dear Watson": the undertones of a myth often improve on the original.

More unusually we find undertones in the life stories of a certain type of man - hard to define, impossible to explain, but something sensed. Edward Fitzgerald (1809-1883) is the example given here and he too felt the sadness and pathos of small and fleeting things - the glint of sunlight on a leaf, caught and then gone: the greenness outside his bedroom window, scent of hay, sound of whetstone on scythe, the roses already passing away, birdsong, "church bells, the wind in the trees, rattle of ropes, the sharp hiss of the sea".

CHAPTER III

Culture and the Expanded Mind

I have summed up the message of Platonism as an act of faith that "if we live as we ought we shall see things as they are, and if we see things as they are we shall live life as we ought".

Without what we call our debt to Greece we should have neither our religion nor our philosophy nor our science nor our literature nor our education nor our politics. We should be mere barbarians.

DEAN INGE

Matthew Arnold (1822-1888) never sensed eternity, nor was he a Platonist or even a theist, but he was one of best advocates of the expanded mind in English, particularly in *Culture and Anarchy* (1869). He was a poet for only about ten years, and that at a time of crisis and change - we can read this, in fact, in his own poetry: he wrote *Dover Beach,* about the ebb and ending of Christianity, in 1851 when he was twenty-nine and on his honeymoon: This world ...

Hath really neither joy, nor love, nor light,
Nor certitude, nor peace, nor help for pain;

And we are here as on a darkling plain
Swept with confused alarms of struggle and flight,
Where ignorant armies clash by night.

Four years later he wrote *Stanzas from the Grande Chartreuse*:

Thinking of his own Gods, a Greek
In pity and mournful awe might stand
Before some fallen Runic stone -
For both were faiths, and both are gone.

Wandering between two worlds, one dead
The other powerless to be born,
With nowhere yet to rest my head
Like these, on earth I wait forlorn.

Then he married a judge's daughter, became an inspector of schools (hours in gaslit railway station waiting rooms), and set about changing the English* who, he thought, had three problems: a general cultural impoverishment and an absence of "right reason": an addiction to liberty, a "passion for doing what one likes" which led to relativism and fragmentation. The third problem was yet to be - the coming of mass democracy for which few of the new electorate (or the old for that matter) were ready. His answers were Hellenism, learning, Hebraism*, stripped down Christianity, Government-controlled schools, and a religion of poetry.

Hellenism is the way of clarity and learning, of grace and mental sunlight, serenity, "radiance and aerial ease". Hellenism is "sweetness and light" (beauty and the intellect - by which he meant pure reason, *not* a sense of eternity or the unseen). Hellenism is also the foundation of "culture", an overview of "the best of what's been thought and said": with it we overcome narrowness and bigotry to see life steadily and see it whole, as Sophocles did: "see the object as it really is". "Hellenism speaks of thinking clearly, seeing things in their essence and beauty, as a grand and precious feat for man to achieve." "Culture is not a having and a getting but a growing and becoming." It raises the Ordinary Self to the Best Self, fully actualised and self-harmonious. It's active, working away unseen inside, illuminating the world. Happiness is the outcome, and happiness is an indicator of deep genuineness, authenticity and truth.

Arnold's ideas in turn stemmed originally from sermons which John Newman (now a saint but then a vicar) preached to undergraduates every Sunday in St Mary's on the High Street in Oxford. Then in 1851, the year of *Dover Beach*, Newman was appointed Rector of the new Catholic University in Dublin. The bishops wanted their university to turn out money-making professionals but Newman wanted something else - he explained what in *The Idea of a University* (1852). What is the chief characteristic of a properly functioning healthy mind? "Illumination," was his best answer: the intellect should shine with an inner light - it should be lit, illuminated, luminous. Luminosity comes when the intellect has an over-all understanding or overview of its own civilisation - its history, philosophy, literature, art. "We perfect our nature, not by undoing it, but by adding to it what is more than nature, and directing it towards aims higher than its own."

The well-stocked mind, moreover, is a good thing in its own right. "Nothing is excellent, beautiful, perfect, desirable for its own sake, but it overflows, and spreads a likeness of itself all around it. A great good will impart a great good. A good mind is a good to all around it. The cultivated intellect brings with it a power and grace to every work."

Newman in turn owed something to Coleridge who argued that culture is the spiritual software resting on a mind furnished with the right kind of knowledge and which in turn rests on the hardware of civilisation - nowadays computers, coffee shops and plumbing, among other things. Without the spirituality bequeathed by culture nobody can be fully human or free. The Clerisy, a word he made up, are the learned guardians, expanders and passers-on of culture. Newman, therefore, essentially argued that the Clerisy should be lodged in universities to pass on this Greek-based culture intact: other more materialist studies - geology or law, physics or psychology - can be tacked on later.

Arnold, and others, used the world Clerisy well into the 19th century and the idea, if not the term, lived on in other late Victorians. For T S Eliot, tradition meant internalising the whole history of our civilisation, from Homer onwards, the whole held timelessly and simultaneously in the mind. He published *Notes Towards a Definition of Culture* in 1948: culture is best described as that which makes life worthwhile. It can't be consciously constructed, it's an unconscious growth in a homogeneous society with enough internal differences to create creative frictions. Religion is also vital - but there's a problem: primitive cultures have simple religions, those of higher civilisations are more complex, making belief harder. But high culture is essential because it makes people "bigger and better" (a phrase of Ruskin's). Eliot feared low culture was winning, even in 1948.

CHAPTER IV

Christianity

If Christianity goes, the whole of our culture goes. Then you must start painfully again, and you cannot put on a new culture ready made. You must wait for the grass to grow to feed the sheep to give the wool out of which your new coat will be made.s You must pass through many centuries of barbarism. We should not live to see the new culture, nor would our great-great-great-grandchildren: and if we did not one of us would happy in it.

T S ELIOT

Secularists ask impatiently what Christianity has done or proposes to do to make mankind happier, by which they mean more comfortable. The answer is ... that Christianity increases the wealth of the world by creating new values.

The Christian Church was the last great creative achievement of the classical culture.

DEAN INGE

Platonism meets Christianity most closely in St Paul, a preacher before there was a religion to preach. "St. Paul was a Jew of the

Dispersion," says Inge, "not of Palestine, and the Christianity to which he was converted was the Christianity of Stephen, not of James the Lord's brother". We can trace his growth in the Epistles, letters he wrote to wayward congregations he'd set up in Greek cities around the eastern Med. (The first Letter probably dates from around the year 50, two decades after the Crucifixion, and fifteen or so years before St Mark's Gospel.) In Thessalonians he's still Pharaisical: the Messiah will soon be here, striding on clouds of glory. But then he reached a purely mystical Religion of the Spirit based, like Platonism, on an experience which is itself salvation. Nobody seems to have been aware of this until the end of the 19th century when it became the thesis of Auguste Sabatier's *Religions of Authority and the Religion of the Spirit* (1904): "Two systems of theology still confront one another: the theology of authority and the theology of experience."

When St Paul talks about the old man dying and the new being born, he means getting rid of the ugliness of ego by stopping thought to let the beatific vision break through. The vision, as far as I can see, is of the peace that passeth understanding embodied in some way in Christ. Presumably Paul was culturally locked out of the *Is* by the concrete concept of the Judaic *Am* - a concept we look at more deeply in the next chapter. Some say he thought of Christ as a created angelic spirit raised to the highest level below the Father. Jesus first becomes God in St John, written in the 90s, some forty years after Paul began writing.

"In the conflict about the nature of the future life," Inge goes on, "it was the Greek eschatology which prevailed over the Jewish. St. Paul's famous declaration, "We look not at the things which are seen, but at the things which are not seen; for the things which are seen are temporal, but the things which are not seen are eternal", is pure Platonism and quite alien to Jewish thought. Judaic Christianity was a local affair, and had a very short life".

Paul also began to turn Christianity into a Greek Mystery

Religion. "It is useless to deny," Inge writes, "that St. Paul regarded Christianity as, at least on one side, a mystery-religion. Why else should he have used a number of technical terms which his readers would recognise at once as belonging to the mysteries? Why else should he repeatedly use the word "mystery" itself, applying it to doctrines distinctive of Christianity, such as the resurrection with a "spiritual body," the relation of the Jewish people to God, and, above all, the mystical union between Christ and Christians? … It was as a mystery-religion that Europe accepted Christianity."

The Greek mysteries were to Paul what Orphism may have been to Plato: a way of boosting the chances of experiencing eternity and making it repeatable. They began in the Axial Age as a way of ensuring salvation. First came Dionysus preaching salvation through debauchery, then Orphism, then the Pythagoreans and then, in the 5th century BC, the Athenian Eleusinian* mysteries about which we know quite a bit since they're weren't too closed and exclusive. "The three chief characteristics of mystery-religion were, first, rites of purification, both moral and ceremonial; second, the promise of spiritual communion with some deity, who through them enters into his worshippers; third, the hope of immortality, which the Greeks often called "deification", and which was secured to those who were initiated." Inge argues that the early Church turned the rituals of the Mysteries into the eucharist and sacraments, into prayer, art, music, and the scent of incense.

Finally, and less fortunately, in Philippians, Colossians, and Ephesians Paul outlined what became an institutionalised religion: "the Catholic doctrine of the Church as the body of Christ is more prominent than individualistic mysticism". Christianity replaced the fallen Roman Empire: the Pope became the Caesar of the Seven Hills, priests replaced the legions, brooking no dissent. Inge writes: "In the last period of antiquity we feel ourselves in a modern atmosphere, though we can see the shadows closing in. Then for many centuries we are in an alien and barbarous world, in which the most fruitful part of European culture seems to have died."

St Thomas Aquinas (1225-1274) Aristotelianised - or de-Platonised - the Church in the 13th century. For Platonists, the body is merely the carrier of the mind and soul. In Aristotelian Christianity, the carrier matters as much as the carried, since body/soul being inextricably linked.

The Reformation might have uncovered the Pauline Religion of the Spirit if either Luther or Calvin had been remotely Platonist by temperament or experience. But St Paul's *Romans* told Luther that faith was all you need to be saved. (The Church of England was a political solution for a people who'd long felt a national kinship: Alfred already called himself king of the *Angelcynn* - English kin - in 886 after taking London from the Danes. England has been a unitary kingdom since 927 when King Alfred's grandson, Athelstan, united the country in roughly its present borders.) Inge called the Reformation the German Renaissance since it came out of Scholasticism and Church philosophy. The Reformation, in fact, squandered the gains of the Renaissance because it favoured a book, not personal experience. Inge always maintained that the North never understood Mediterranean Christianity where the old gods lived on as saints. Reformers de-paganised religion and rid it of Roman Imperialism. They elevated the Old Testament without being aware of how remote it was, and alien. All the same, Protestantism is in essence individualist, inward and universalist not collectivist and rule-bound*. Humanism was one outcome: bibliolatry is less of a hindrance to it than infallibility. The Reformation in England also supported the Industrial Revolution by giving people permission to make money, a sign of divine favour and a better way of spreading the Gospel. A thousand years of theocratic stagnation ended, new nation states evolved, science and learning took off, the secular became dominant.

CHAPTER V

Limits and the Unlimited

*The mystic holds these views because he has lived through
an experience which has forced him to this attitude of mind;
but his experience does not convince any one else.*

CAROLINE SPURGEON*

*If you are quite without the gift of devotion, it is a defect
in our make-up, like the lack of power to appreciate music
or poetry. It is a defect to be deplored, and to be made good
if possible. For if the spiritual world is real, and all about
us, it is a misfortune if we cannot come into contact with
it. My favourite philosopher Plotinus thinks we can all get
into touch with it: we have only to call into activity a faculty
"which all possess but few use".*

*Religion can only be understood from inside. What are
called "evidences" will not help us much: but when the mystic
tells us what he has seen, we may believe him.*

*Accordingly, since the psychologist has debarred himself from
explaining mysticism by philosophy (in the older sense), he
is practically obliged to explain it by pathology.*

In *The Future of an Illusion* (1927) Sigmund Freud (1856-1939)
argued that religion had had its day and science was taking over.
The old deities of nature had evolved into a single God whose
job was to protect believers but now, in turn, the newcomer's
time was up. Freud sent a copy of his book to Romain Rolland
(1866-1944)*. You're wrong, Rolland replied: religion is based
on "a sensation of eternity", on the unbounded and unlimited,
on a sense of the "oceanic". No, said Freud. I've never experienced those things and neither have you. All you experience is
"a regression to an earlier state: that of the infant at the breast."
Religion comes about because of "the infant's sense of helpless-
ness … the need for a father's protection". That oceanic feeling
is the need to deny that the world is dangerous.

Plato influenced Freud in at least one way - the Id, Ego,
and Superego are clearly copies of the Platonic tripartite soul,
the charioteer and his two horses in the *Phaedrus* - but Freud
was a materialist who "mistook the limits of his vision for the
limits of the world". His reaction to Rolland would be even
more common today: the West has long since lost any awareness
of the gap between Platonists and Incompletes. Nowadays, in
fact, we're allowed to believe only if we have material evidence.
William Kingdon Clifford, who died aged only thirty-three
in 1879 may have been behind this. He was a Cambridge

mathematician, originator of Clifford algebra, who wrote: "It is wrong, always, everywhere and for anyone, to believe anything on insufficient evidence." What evidence he had for believing that is, of course, another matter.

Half the youth of the Anglosphere now go to university. How often do you hear or read "I've been to uni where I was taught to think for myself"? That teaching comes with a Critical Thinking checklist: can you trust the source of this belief/opinion? What evidence/data/statistics uphold it? Is the proposer qualified to have an opinion? Does he/she have something to gain from spreading this belief? What assumptions are here? What biases? Is the conclusion logically obtained? What are the practical downsides of accepting this opinion? What are the opposing points of view? Is the conclusion falsifiable, based on reason (not emotion), does the explanation truly explain?

Critical Thinking is a more formulated kind of Socratic Questioning, Plato's *elenchus*, one which Sophists can use to disprove, damage, debunk, deride, denigrate and even destroy those with wrong opinions. It's essential for straight thinking, of course, but less so if the thinker misuses it to defend or promote ideas and opinions emotionally derived and driven. It's also reductionist and so not designed to see life steadily and see it whole. A critical thinker might find that Platonism scores badly in these tests: there's no empirical evidence for it, no measurable facts as Hume put it, no statistics or testable data. But the questions are pointless because the ultimate answers are beyond the scope of thinking or logic (which in any case collapses at the quantum level).

With dualist religions such as Christianity believers have to prove that God exists. Without proof you need faith. With monist philosophies such as Platonism, on the other hand, disbelievers have to prove that the experience is false. Faith or belief doesn't come into it until and unless they can prove that what is experienced is not real - not really what the experiencer thinks it is. Proving God's existence, in other words, is objective: falsifying eternity is subjective.

So conditioned are we in the West to see nothing but matter that the ability to view the world from a different angle is hard or even impossible. But some people can switch and then, for them, it's a bit like looking at one of those drawings which are also optical illusions: two heads facing each other flick into a vase, or an old woman flips into a young one. Best of all is Jastrow's duck which flops into a rabbit: in the West, materialism is the default duck but it can turn into the immaterialist rabbit and, once it does, you never see the world the same way again.

CHAPTER VI

Last Things

*The time for promiscuous and experimental reading is before
we have quite found ourselves. Sooner or later, we arrive
at conclusions which for us are the only possible conclusions.
They would not suit everybody, but for us they are the truth.
Having reached this stage, it is waste of time to study
writers with whom we have no sympathy.*

*Alike in religion and philosophy the important question is
not whether God exists, but what we mean when we speak
of God.*

DEAN INGE

Good outcomes are arguments for the truth.

WM. JAMES

*Metaphysics is the finding of bad reasons for what we believe
on instinct; but to find those reasons is no less an instinct.*

F H BRADLEY

Platonism has a simple eschatology - all will be well, not in this life of course but when it ends. That's the conclusion you come to when you experience eternity which is beauty, peace and pure consciousness (a kind of Aristotelian Unmoved Mover perhaps). The soul is what senses eternity and so is also eternal and as such can't die, but neither can it have a personal afterlife since it doesn't have a self which needs time, and in eternity there is none.

On the other hand, this is scarcely a God fit for the fox-hole or the forlorn - for that we need some kind of Christian Platonism or Platonic Christianity. What we call Being or eternity, Plato called *Ho Estin - The It Is*. The Judaic Jehovah is *I Am*. The *Is* is part of nature, the *Am* is above it. The *Is* is abstract, aetherial, immaterial, impersonal, changeless, spaceless, the realm of beauty. The *Am* is exoteric, personal, wholly other. The *Am* is a choice, the *Is* is an experience.

We know there's such a thing as consciousness (ours) so why can't consciousness re-appear at a higher level, more far seeing, closer to ultimate reality, something we can call God, a superior presence in the material cosmos? Eckhart, the 14th century Dominican friar, distinguished between God and the Godhead. God is a mountain on the plains of the Godhead where we are knolls or hillocks. The Godhead is the *Is*, God is the *Am*, a lesser aspect of eternity but higher than our own.

Platonism is also immaterialist - the immaterial (eternity) is primary and matter is held in "like a thought". There's no evidence that matter exists independently of non-matter, or that matter makes non-matter. If the immaterial is immortal then so is the self since it's conscious of its own existence and is therefore not made of matter. Is *Am*-the-Mountain the self's final dwelling place, in the old phrase?

But what about the gross imperfections of this species, its tiresome or terrifying flaws ranging from envy to gulags and genocide? Perhaps Origen (c185-c254), Bishop of Caesarea, was right - the self carries on evolving until it graduates into a higher state of being. In Dante's *Purgatory,* Arnaut Daniel, the troubadour, dives gladly back into the flame to be refined, like gold: "Remember my pain, I pray you, when you reach the summit of the stair".

Origen also had a Hell in his eschatology but it was time-limited, designed to shut down when the last soul graduated into Heaven since the everlasting torture of flawed creatures is untenable - human pity or compassion, for example, would make the created greater than the creator. The concept of Hell, a relic of ancient cruelty, also contradicts the Christian concepts of love and forgiveness.

Origen, again, argued that Christianity may not be literally true, but spiritually it most certainly is. He read the New Testament as an allegory. Christianity can therefore be accepted as a myth, a story which tells a truth: Christ symbolises eternity-incarnate while the Crucifixion and Resurrection graphically demonstrate the immortality of the soul, along with the power of suffering, self-sacrifice, forgiveness and love. You can be an atheist - in the sense of disbelieving in a Maker - and still be a Christian Platonist.

Oscar Wilde even thought the miracles were real: they came from "the charm of Christ's character" - bringing "peace to souls in anguish", making the deaf hear the Voice of Love, the blind to see the Beauty which is love. "Evil passions fled at his approach." The multitude on the mountain were too engrossed to feel hungry. Water could taste like wine in his presence because Christ symbolises eternity.

But even if all of this is wrong and nothing but matter exists, belief in an afterlife would still be worthwhile because of the benefit it bestows. "The consolation of imaginary things is not imaginary consolation", as Roger Scruton put it. Practical reason also has something to say: look inside your mind and sample both eternity and its absence (often a void colonised by loneliness, aloneness, isolation and despair). You can turn either way but which is better - the beauty of fullness or the ugliness of emptiness? What do you choose - rage or rest? Bewilderment or what makes life worth living?

Practical reason can't even explain the why and the what of the oddity of here and so has nothing to say about the soul which senses eternity. Those who do experience it never doubt they've touched the very nature of Being itself. So profoundly real is it that they see no reason to impoverish themselves by rejecting something of the greatest value simply because others are blind.

PART TWO

Aspects of Platonism

CHAPTER I

Wordsworth: The Poet and the Contracted Mind

Wordsworth was not only a poet, he was also a seer, a mystic and a practical psychologist with an amazingly subtle mind, and an unusual capacity for feeling; he lived a life of excitement and passion, and he preached a doctrine of magnificence and glory. It was not the beauty of Nature which brought him joy and peace, but the life in Nature. He himself had caught a vision of that life, he knew it and felt it, and it transformed the whole of existence for him.

CAROLINE SPURGEON

The passion for unifying all experience, for seeing unity behind all multiplicity, is the other side of his desire to unify his own personality. This also is an integral part of Wordsworth's creed. He is not really so bent on the perception of beauty as on that of Being, of the one all-pervading Life.

DEAN INGE

He saw Nature and man with new eyes, and his whole work is an attempt to communicate that vision. ... He had

William Wordsworth (1770-1850) is the finest Platonist poet in English and yet although beauty was part of his vision he sank into eternity directly without a go-between. He also wrote all his best poetry in a single Great Decade, 1798 to 1808, beginning when he was a young man of twenty-eight. In those ten years, too, he revolutionised poetry by writing it in the language of common day and using it for social reform, focusing on the poor, the oppressed and dispossessed or - in Hazlitt's words - "a mixed rabble of Botany Bay convicts, female vagrants, gypsies, idiot boys and mad mothers".

He experienced a sense of eternity many times in his childhood in the Lake District, particularly when he ran wild as a schoolboy around Windermere and in the Vale of Esthwaite. He wrote about these mystical events in his autobiographical poem, *The Prelude* (1805), five or six years after they either stopped or eased off. Other Platonist/mystical poems appear in *Lyrical Ballads* (1798) and *Poems* (1807) - particularly *Tintern Abbey* and *Intimations of Immortality*.

In *The Prelude* he tells of his childhood and the good life:

> Fair seed-time had my soul, and I grew up
> Fostered alike by beauty and by fear.

From *Intimations of Immortality*:

> There was a time when meadow, grove, and stream,
> The earth, and every common sight,
> To me did seem
> Apparelled in celestial light.

Poets, he writes, are here to "rectify men's feelings", to make the reader's "feelings more sane, pure and permanent, in short, more consonant to nature, that is, to eternal nature and the great moving spirit of things". In his boyhood and early manhood, he was at one with a cosmos in which there was no creator, no created, because all is uncreated:

> ... in all things now
> I saw one life, and felt that it was joy.

This is from *Tintern Abbey*, in the Wye valley where the river flows between Herefordshire, Gloucestershire and Monmouthshire:

> And I have felt
> A presence that disturbs me with the joy
> Of elevated thoughts; a sense sublime

Of something far more deeply interfused,
Whose dwelling is the light of setting suns,
And the round ocean and the living air,
And the blue sky, and in the mind of man:
A motion and a spirit that impels
All thinking things, all objects of all thought
And rolls through all things.

"I had to push," he writes in prose, "against something that resisted, to be sure there was anything outside of me."

One night when he was twenty-two, still an undergraduate, he climbed Mount Snowdon with two friends in the early morning dark to watch the dawn. A thick mist or cloud covered the lower slopes so that standing above it was like being on the shores of a white sea which filled the bays of the hills and stretched away over the real ocean. A full moon shone in a clear sky. Silence and sound were there together. The noise was of streams pouring down the mountains under the sea-cloud. He felt he was in the presence of a living mind which "feeds upon infinity". Anybody, everybody, would have sensed eternity that early morning on Snowdon but "higher minds" create those experiences all the time out of more daily things.

A meditation rose in me that night
Upon the lonely Mountain when the scene
Had pass'd away, and it appear'd to me
The perfect image of a mighty Mind,
Of one that feeds upon infinity,
That is exalted by an underpresence,
The sense of God, or whatsoe'er is dim
Or vast in its own being.

Sight of course was his dominant sense but sound could work too (apparently he had little sense of smell). He recalls evenings by Windermere when he'd imitate the call of an owl on cupped hands. Owls all around the lake called back: he'd urge them on into wild hooting and echoes. Then they'd stop. In that silence, the outer world slid inside him and he became one with it.

Words had some effect as well. As a boy at Hawkshead he'd walk in the early mornings with a friend reciting poetry together (Gray, mainly it seems, and Goldsmith). In words he found "a passion and a power":

> … Visionary Power
> Attends upon the motions of the winds
> Embodied in the mystery of words.

He believed that poets should - *must* - "see things as they are". *Is, are, am, be,* are important words in Wordsworth, Helen Darbishire points out, because what mystics see is Being itself. "Am" and "Being" are the same thing because ultimately all is one (hence treat the downtrodden with decency and respect).

A sense of under-ness is common to all levels of mystics because the only really important things lie beneath material reality. Wordsworth coined "under-soul", though it's not all that clear what he meant; the unconscious, perhaps (a word introduced into English by Coleridge from the German of Schelling). "Soul-ness" is another Wordsworth coinage: he seems to have meant "spiritual" by it. Great minds, he says, are "exalted by an underpresence". Later, he changed this to "unconsciousness" but the passage in the 1805 *The Prelude* makes it plain he meant a sense of the presence of God.

Even when not about eternity, the work of his great period is suffused with the sadness and repose which Ruskin said are the hallmarks not only of all great poetry but also of the experience of eternity itself. From *Lines Written in Early Spring*:

> To her fair works did nature link
> The human soul that through me ran;
> And much it grieved my heart to think
> What man has made of man.

He also worked out how it's done - by clearing the mind of "little enmities and low desires" until a "wise passiveness" or "happy stillness of mind" is arrived at. Nothing is too big or small to make it happen - from people to love, from dust and grit on the highway to landscape. Once, while crossing the Alps, he suddenly knew that "our being's heart and home is with infinitude" and that this knowledge comes

> ... when the light of sense
> Goes out, but with a flash that has revealed
> The invisible world.

How did he sum up mysticism/Platonism? "Central peace subsisting at the heart of endless agitation." Busyness with the material world is an eternity blocker, he realised. "The world is too much with us" he wrote in a sonnet in 1806; all this "getting and spending" leads nowhere. And he was pre-Ruskin in regretting the passing of the spirituality of the Greeks who saw gods in woods. We all need to

> Have sight of Proteus rising from the sea;
> Or hear old Triton blow his wreathèd horn.

"What is this mysticism?" he also asked. How can matter know non-matter, how can the physical see the unphysical?

Sensibly, he said he didn't know while insisting *something* happens and therefore whatever it is, it exists: *it is*.

> I guess not what this tells of Being past,
> Nor what it augurs of the life to come,
> But so it is.

He called those intense events "spots of time": they work away hidden in the under-soul, or unhidden in the memory, to make life more fully lived. He talks about spots of *remembered* time:

> Those shadowy recollections,
> Which, be they what they may,
> Are yet a fountain light of all our day,
> And yet a master light of all our seeing.

Finally, to hark back a bit, there might be some doubt as to when those spots of time eventually stopped. During the Peninsular War - which began in 1808 and ended in 1814 - Wordsworth and Coleridge used to walk to Dunmail Raise to meet the cart which brought the newspapers. Wordsworth often put his ear to the ground to listen for the rumble of wheels. One evening, as he stood up again, he noticed a star over Helvellyn. It triggered a "sense of the infinite". Why? Because of relaxation following concentration, was his answer.

In 1818, now aged 48, the wrote a poem - *Composed upon an Evening of Extraordinary Splendour and Beauty* - which some think was his last farewell to the mystic event:

> 'Tis past, the visionary splendour fades;
> And night approaches with her shades.

But he'd already said *a* farewell in *Intimations of Immortality* in 1804, aged thirty-four, near the end of his Great Decade:

> Yet now I know, where'er I go,
> That there hath past away a glory from the earth.
>
> Whither is fled the visionary gleam?
> Where is it now, the glory and the dream?
>
> At length the Man perceives it die away,
> And fade into the light of common day.

Yet also in the end:

> Thanks to the human heart by which we live,
> Thanks to its tenderness, its joys, and fears,
> To me the meanest flower that blows can give
> Thoughts that do often lie too deep for tears.

CHAPTER II

De Profundis

Can a Platonist be a Christian without renouncing the philosophy which he has found satisfying, both as an interpretation of the universe as it reveals itself to human experience, and as a rule of life, a path of ascent up the hill of the Lord? I believe that not only is it possible, but that the Christian revelation puts the keystone in the arch, and completes what the long travail of the human spirit, during many centuries of free and unfettered thought, had discovered about the nature of the world in which we live, the laws of God and the whole duty of man.

What is particularly Christian about Christian Platonism is "mainly the identification of the inner light with the Spirit of the living, glorified and indwelling Christ".

DEAN INGE

Oddly enough, we can find an example of Christian Platonism in the last few months of the life of Oscar Wilde (1854-1900), a dandy in velvet breeches ("a poppy and a lily in a Medieval hand"), socialist revolutionary, playwright, Café Royal epigram-matist, wit and raconteur. Four years after writing *The Soul of Man Under Socialism*, Wilde was sent down for sodomy and imprisoned in Reading jail. He was a man least able to handle life in a late Victorian prison (1895/97) yet his best work - *De Profundis* - came out of it. Richard Ellmann, his biographer, said *De Profundis* was a kind of dramatic monologue, a love letter to Bosie, Lord Alfred Douglas, the immediate cause of his downfall. It's much more than that. Half is about Bosie's wrong doing and an attempt to fix things between them. A lot, immodestly, is about his own genius - it's an "elegy for lost greatness," as he put it, calling himself the symbol of art and culture for his age. "The gods have given me almost everything. I had genius, a distinguished name, high social position, brilliancy, intellectual daring ... I altered the lives of men and the colours of things: there was nothing I said that did not make people wonder."

But in the same book, he also goes deeper. Christ "ranks with the poets" and his life story is greater than the entire "cycle of Greek Tragedy". Nothing in all literature compares to the Passion: supper (with a betrayer), "anguish in the quiet moonlit olive-garden," a false friend to betray, a true friend to run away, loneliness, submission, acceptance, a magistrate washing away his own guilt, a "coronation of sorrow", crucifixion before his mother and the disciple he loved, soldiers dicing for his cloak, a terrible death (giving the world its most "eternal symbol"), a tomb, an empty tomb, a resurrection. Nothing in art is remotely like it and only the imaginative can see it at all. The life of Christ is Sorrow and Beauty made one.

In jail, Wilde finally understood the essence of Christianity: love, forgiveness, self-sacrifice and sorrow. Love is vital. By love, he says, "we become wiser than we know, better than we feel, nobler than we are: by which we can see Life as a whole: by which, and by which alone, we can understand others in their real as in their ideal relations. Only what is fine, and finely conceived, can feed Love. But anything will feed Hate." "Hate blinds people." Wilde also quotes Renan who, in *Vie de Jesus*, tells us that love "was the lost secret of the world for which the wise had been looking, and that it was only through love that one could approach either the heart of the leper or the Feet of God".

"At all costs," Wilde said on being sent down, "I must keep Love in my heart. If I go to prison without Love what will become of my soul?"

"When one comes in contact with the soul," Wilde goes on, "it makes one as simple as a child". To do so you have to ditch everything - possessions and passions and everything you've ever learned. Few meet the soul. "Most people are other people. Their thoughts are someone else's opinion, their life is a mimicry, their passions a quotation. Christ is not merely the supreme individualist but he was the first in History."

Wilde in jail learned humility - defined as the "frank acceptance of all experience". But he also learned the importance, not of being earnest, but of suffering and sorrow. "Suffering is the means by which we exist, because it is the only means by which we become conscious of existing." We have to remember past suffering as evidence of a "continued identity".

"Where there is Sorrow, there is holy ground."

He also learned about forgiveness and repentance. You have to forgive in order to pluck bitterness out of the heart - "one cannot always keep an adder in one's breast to feed on one" - because only then can you become self-realised.

But he also became a kind of Platonist: self-realisation, the becoming of a complete individual, he also saw as essential.

"The essence of thought, as the essence of life, is growth."

"Self-culture is the true ideal of man."

"Where self-development has ceased to be the ideal, the intellectual standard is instantly lowered and, often, ultimately lost."

Mechanical people know where they want to go - and go there - but those who seek self-realisation don't know where they're going and furthermore they never get there because each of us is a mystery and the soul is ultimately unknowable. "My nature is seeking a fresh mode of self-realisation. And the first thing I have got to do is free myself from any possibility of feeling against you," he writes in his book-length letter to Bosie.

"The external things of life seem to me now of no importance at all. You can see to what intensity of individualism I have arrived, or am arriving rather for the journey is long."

But Wilde also saw the power of beauty. He agreed with Plato on education: the child should be so brought up that "the beauty of material things may prepare his soul for the reception of the beauty that is spiritual." Plato said: "Love of beauty is the true aim of education". Education should provide an overview which lets you see, and so choose, the good.

Art isn't big in Plato but it is in Platonism which can be called "the cult of beauty". Plato was the first to feel "the desire to know the connection between Beauty and Truth." Beauty is spiritual in its own right and so can spiritualise art. Art for art's sake isn't enough: art has to be about of something bigger and better than any kind of self. He even sided with Ruskin - without saying so - over Gothic architecture. The Gothic gave us Chartres, Arthurian legends, St Francis, Giotto, Dante. The Renaissance gave us Petrarch, Raphael, Palladianism, French tragedies, St Paul's, Pope's poetry "and everything made from without and by dead rules, and does not spring from within through some spirit informing it".

"Still, I am conscious now that behind all this Beauty there is some Spirit hidden of which the painted forms and shapes are but modes of manifestation, and it is with this Spirit that I desire to become in harmony. The Mystical in Art, the Mystical in Life, the Mystical in Nature. It is absolutely necessary for me to find it somewhere."

CHAPTER III

Old Man in a Dry Month

The life of Edward Fitzgerald, particularly in his later years, is I think a source of undertones and fragments although he is - or was until recently - remembered mainly as the translator of *The Rubaiyat of Omar Khayyam*, the 12th century Persian eulogy of wine and hedonistic fatalism, as far from Fitzgerald's own character as you can get.

He was born a Purcell, in 1809, in Suffolk, as A C Benson tells us in his 1905 biography. Fitzgerald's parents were first cousins : both were Anglo-Irish. John Purcell was a descendant of Oliver Cromwell: his wife of the Earls of Kildare. In 1818 she became the richer of the two, through an inheritance, upon which Purcell changed all their names to hers. (Edward never liked it.) Between them they owned estates in Suffolk, Sussex, Northamptonshire, Lancashire, and Ireland. They had eight children. Edward was seventh.

John FitzGerald (né Purcell), Member of Parliament for Seaford in Sussex, seems to have been a bit feckless, eventually ruining himself through his own folly in digging for coal on his Lancashire estate. His wife, says Benson, was superb and majestic, with a haughty face, eagle nose, and thin mouth. She was such a leading light in London society she rarely saw her children as they grew up in a Jacobean mansion on a FitzGerald estate near Woodbridge in Suffolk. Later writers blame his childhood unhappiness - the whippings, the absence of his cold, imperious mother - as well as his gayness (at a time when it had to be denied or hidden) for his later eccentricity. Benson, a fellow-Victorian who was also gay, disagreed - or rather these things never occurred to him in the first place. He put it all down to temperament. Fitzgerald's childhood was happy, he claims, full of incident and adventure: the boy knew Paris, loved the sea, the theatre, books, and the countryside, huge tracts of which his family owned. He was a lifelong collector of friends and he made them early and late throughout his life. "I am an idle fellow," he said of himself many years later, "of a very ladylike turn of sentiment: and my friendships are more like loves, I think."

Fitzgerald began making friends as a small child at Woodbridge on the River Deben. Major Moor was a stout old Indian Army man in a white hat several sizes too big, carrying a cane cut from the timber of HMS *Royal George.* He was available at all times for walks with the boy. They shared a delight in Suffolk dialect. The Major also collected Eastern gods. Squire Jenny, short and jolly with big ears, was a not untypical Victorian eccentric who let snow blow in through his ever open windows to drift in piles on his uncarpeted floors. His sister kept house, parsimoniously.

In 1818, Fitzgerald was sent to King Edward VI Grammar School in Bury St Edmunds. James Spedding, who later edited the works of Francis Bacon*, was there and they stayed friends for life. In 1826 Fitzgerald went to Trinity College, Cambridge. Thackeray was there: towards the end of his own life Thackeray said FitzGerald was his oldest and best friend - in spite of the fact that he was an extreme extravert (who in the end could write only in public places) while FitzGerald was the exact opposite. A year or two later FitzGerald met the three Tennyson boys. Asked when he was nearing his own end who had been the friend he loved most, Alfred, Lord Tennyson replied: "Why, old Fitz, to be sure."

At University, Fitzgerald settled into his lifelong dilettante ways, pottering, dabbling, picking up and putting down the classics, water colours, music, poetry, without any system or aim. Already, too, he was unkempt, dishevelled and badly clothed. When his mother called (in a coach and four) he had no boots to wear to meet her. He was, of course, well off (Carlyle claimed he gave Tennyson at least three hundred pounds a year at this time). After graduating, he began a drifting life; parties, visits, travel, breakfasts, the theatre. He was in Paris with Thackeray who shouldn't have been there, and lied about it.

Two new friendships at this time were to bring him pain and trouble later on: William Browne, a hearty riding, shooting and fishing type, and Bernard Barton, a Quaker who worked in a bank in Woodbridge. Barton was a poet and art collector (he had two Cotmans). He also had a daughter, Lucy, the direct cause of Fitzgerald's future grief.

Then, in 1837, still only twenty-eight, FitzGerald settled permanently in Suffolk where his father had recently bought Boulge Park by the River Deben. FitzGerald took over a two-roomed lodge in the grounds. He had a bust of Shakespeare, a dog, cat, Beauty Bob (a parrot), and two servants: an old soldier who'd served at Waterloo, and his snuff-taking wife. All that and a barrel of beer. The place was a shambles, and he was unshaven and slovenly. "What will become of him in this world?" Spedding asked.

The coast of Suffolk is flat and the River Deben is tidal as far as Woodbridge although it's around ten miles from the sea. (The name has more to do with Woden than with timber.) In the 16th and 17th centuries it was a ship-building sea port. By Queen Victoria's time it was a back-water, visited maybe by Thames barges and yawls with cargoes of grain for the tide mill. In 1859 the railway reached the town, but to this day it isn't all that easy to get to.

George Crabbe was the eighteenth-century poet of that coast and his son, also called George, was vicar of Bredfield and was yet another eccentric: his daughters emptied his pockets before they let him out of the house to stop him giving all their money away. He quickly became another good friend. It's said, though it seems unlikely, that FitzGerald proposed to the eldest daughter. If he did, she said no, although she was with him when he died, in 1883, in her father's house. That, though, was nearly forty years away.

Meanwhile he continued an annual summertime drift for the next ten years. Part of most summers he spent with Browne in Bedfordshire. Once he visited Dublin with him to see his own Purcell cousins and meet the novelist Maria Edgeworth (in Edgeworthtown) whose brother he'd known in Cambridge. Once, in London, he took a drive with Dickens, Thackeray, and Tennyson: all four in the same carriage.

In 1842, now thirty-three, he met Carlyle. Carlyle had recently been with Dr Arnold to the Civil War battlefield at Naseby in Northamptonshire researching his book, *Cromwell*. Cromwell, of course, was one of FitzGerald's ancestors and, as it happened, FitzGerald's father owned the estate where the battle had taken place in 1645. He'd erected an obelisk to mark the site of the fiercest fighting. Unfortunately it was in the wrong place and Carlyle and Arnold had got themselves excited over a piece of ground across which neither Cromwell's Ironsides nor Prince Rupert's Cavaliers had ever ridden. FitzGerald obliged them by pointing out the real site, even digging up the bones of fallen musketeers and pikemen. "In the intervals of the task," Benson writes, "he read the Georgics, and watched the horses plodding and clanking out to the harvest-fields, up the lanes with their richly twined tapestries of briony and bind-weed."

It was around this time, too, that Fitzgerald, a lifelong agnostic, came closest to accepting Christianity. His oldest brother, John, whose eccentricity verged on madness, was a fervent evangelical given to threatening country folk with eternal terror. His friend, a Reverend Matthews of Bedford, was a hell-fire revivalist preacher of some power. Like Wesley, like Bunyan, Matthew preached in the open air, blowing a trumpet to attract the crowds. Sometimes he baptised converts in the lake which fed the canal near Naseby - "His sermons shook my soul", though the effect didn't last.

A new friendship in 1846 with the man who introduced him to Farsi and Omar Khayyam had a more lasting effect. Edward Cowell was the twenty-year-old son of an Ipswich corn merchant. Benson says he was shy, amusing, modest, simple, and deeply religious. He married an older woman of private means. He spoke Spanish, Sanskrit and Farsi (or Persian as it was then more commonly called). FitzGerald visited the Cowells in Ipswich where they would sit in the garden (with its monkey puzzle tree and path leading to a mill) reading Spanish, Persian, and Greek. Mrs Cowell wrote poetry, FitzGerald criticised it. When they moved to Oxford, Cowell came across a manu-script in the Bodleian of Omar Khayyam's verses written in purple-black ink on yellow paper powdered all over with gold. He gave a transcript to FitzGerald. All his fame was to be tied up in the poem yet, typically, he did nothing with it for another ten years. Benson, in fact, suggests it was only the traumas of the 1850s - FitzGerald's worst decade emotionally - which got him writing at all.

Just before Barton died, in 1849, the now forty year old FitzGerald promised to care for his daughter, Lucy. Lucy took this to mean marriage: FitzGerald didn't but, diffident as ever, didn't make it plain. As usual he put off a decision, for six years in this case. Meanwhile, his father's digging for coal on his Lancashire estate ended in 1851 with his own ruin and that of Squire Jenny who'd invested in him. Both old men died within a few months. The Squire's ancient woods were felled to pay off his debts. FitzGerald's allowance stopped but, because his mother had always been the richer of the two parents, it didn't affect him too badly although perhaps the temporary drop in income induced him to agree to marry Lucy because he couldn't afford to pay an allowance. The wedding, however, was still five years away.

Even then things were not too bad (FitzGerald never had really hard times). His brother John, the evangelical, inherited Boulge. To get away from him FitzGerald moved into lodgings with a farmer, Job Smith, in Farlingay Hall. There were just the five of them: Job, his wife and son, and a maid who dropped the tea pot when she curtsied in the morning. FitzGerald was contented enough. He bought a boat. Carlyle invited himself to stay. "I hope to get to Farlingay not long after four o'clock," he wrote, "and have a quiet mutton chop in due time and have a ditto pipe or pipes: nay, I could even bathe if there was any sea water left in the evening."

In 1854 Fitzgerald's mother died leaving him an income of around a thousand pounds a year at a time when you could raise a family on a hundred. Two years later the Cowells sailed for India and the long-put-off marriage to Lucy took place in Chichester followed by a honeymoon in Brighton and domesticity in Great Portland Street, narrow and canyon-like, in London. The new Mrs FitzGerald craved dinner parties, calling cards and stately drives in the park while her husband was a dyed-in-the-wool rustic eccentric and at forty-seven too old to change his ways. They separated after a fortnight, then tried living together again in a house overlooking Regent's Park. FitzGerald was utterly depressed but as always shied away from rows and arguments. They then tried Yarmouth, after which FitzGerald gave up - he just never went back to her. (Years later they passed each other in Lowestoft but he was too embarrassed to speak.) She had an allowance and eventually settled in Croydon, then a village outside London. "I am very much to blame," he said later, "both on the score of stupidity in taking so wrong a step, and want of courageous principle in not making the best of it when taken. She was born to rule," he added.

By now his friends were growing old. Crabbe died, probably of a stroke, in 1857. William Browne (perhaps the man he loved most) was crushed by his horse on the hunting field. FitzGerald went to Browne's house in Bedfordshire but at first squeamishly shrank from seeing him. When he did, his friend was barely able to speak or move his hands. He died after nine weeks of paralysed agony.

It was in 1857 in the middle of all this that Fitzgerald turned to Omar Khayyam and his *Rubaiyat* (the word simply means quatrains). His Spanish was shaky, his Persian worse and without Cowell the translation would probably never have got done. He questioned him by mail in India and even then said: "I am not always quite certain of getting the right sow by the ear". He kept a list of queries as he worked through the day. By 1859, when he was fifty, the book was ready. First he offered a few hand-picked verses to *Fraser's*, a magazine for family reading. The editor kept the manuscript for a whole year without replying. FitzGerald then printed two hundred and fifty copies, anonymously, sending most of them to Bernard Quaritch's bookshop in London. Quaritch sold not a single copy for two years until he dumped them in the penny box on the pavement outside. A man called Whitley Stokes bought two for Rossetti and Richard Burton, the orientalist and explorer. Rossetti bought some for Browning and Swinburne. Swinburne bought them for Burne-Jones and George Meredith. In time, Ruskin got a copy. He wrote to the unknown author: "I do not know in the least who you are but I do with all my soul pray you to find and translate some more of Omar Khayyam." Apparently he asked Burne-Jones to post the letter, though of course B-J knew no more about the anonymous author than he did. Ruskin's letter was delivered twelve years later.

In time *The Rubaiyat* became the best selling translation of a poem in English, possibly the best selling poem in English ever. Omar Khayyam Clubs sprang up all over England and America. Conan Doyle, Edmund Gosse and Arthur Pinero belonged to the same one in London. They were pretty lively places by all accounts. Chesterton thought the book was wicked. Browning wrote *Rabbi Ben Ezra* in reply to it, it's said. As late as the 1950s young men got it off by heart. It is "Savage against Destiny", FitzGerald said of it, "Epicurean in its Pathos." It is what everybody feels at the bottom of their hearts. Benson thought it the most beautiful expression of agnosticism, and the Epicureanism which comes with it.

It made no difference to FitzGerald's life. In 1860, now fifty-one, he moved into rooms above the gun-maker's shop in Woodbridge market. Job Smith moved to Sutton Hoo where an Anglo-Saxon burial ship would be found seventy-odd years later in the 1930s. FitzGerald bought a sea-going yacht called *The Scandal* (scandal being the staple of conversation in Woodbridge), marvelling at how his skipper never stopped smiling though the father of twins. He took to the water, he said, because the country all around was the graveyard of his friends, and the new generation of landowners was destroying the landscape to make money. Sailing to Aldburgh was a favourite trip. He still delighted in the speech of country people: a sailor said of his boat that she "go like a wiolin" and "all is calm as a clock" after a gale had dropped.

In 1864 he bought a farmhouse near Woodbridge and then, typically, left it empty for ten years, apart from workmen who added rooms and walls and then knocked them again at Fitzgerald's whim. Six acres were planted with a wood. That year too he made a friend of a Lowestoft fisherman called Posh Fletcher. "This is altogether the Greatest Man I have known," he said, idealising him as a leader of men of the finest Anglian type. "A man," FitzGerald added, "of simplicity of soul, justice of thought, tenderness of nature, a gentleman of Nature's grandest type." ("It must be confessed," Benson said, "that a good deal of sentimentality was wasted over this sea-lion.") FitzGerald built Posh a herring lugger, *The Meum and Tuum*.

Fitzgerald's brother, John, still master of Boulge, grew odder and odder, more fervent in his preaching. He kept a clock in every room then rang for his valet when he wanted to know the time. But Cowell, now Professor of Sanskrit in Cambridge, had come back from India and their friendship picked up again. In the 1870s, what zest Fitzgerald ever had for life was fading. He was cheered for a while by the diagnosis of a heart disease which might take him off in an instant. His old friend Spedding finally brought his work on Bacon to an end. "I always look upon old Spedding's as one of the most wasted lives I know," Fitzgerald said.

Not all his friends were men. He loved the actress Fanny Kemble (1809-1893) "sincerely", if not her acting on the stage. The affection was mutual: in 1875, when they were both six-ty-six, she wrote an article for the *Atlantic Monthly* so fulsome that he pasted paper over some of the worst paragraphs. Around this time, as well, he moved into his farmhouse, propelled by eviction from his lodgings. His landlord, Mr Berry, got engaged to a widow. "Old Berry would now have to be called Old Gooseberry," Fitz observed. The widow got to hear of it and he had to go. On eviction day she stood at the foot of the stairs calling up: "Be firm, Berry! Remind him of what he called you."

In the farmhouse, he lived in the downstairs parlour, divided by folding doors. The organ, which he played from memory with-out sheet music, was in the hall. The living room was his library. The rest of the house, with added rooms, was furnished and open at all times to his nieces, though they rarely met. By now he was very set in his ways. Benson says of him: "FitzGerald's habits were absolutely simple; his only plan of action was to do what he liked, and not be bothered. In earlier years he had rambled further afield; but in the quiet days at Woodbridge or Lowestoft, he would spend the morning over books and papers, or write a leisurely letter; he would stroll about, looking at flowers and trees, listening to the voices of birds, talking to his simple acquaintances. Sometimes he would go out in a boat, and gossip with the boatmen. He seems to have had no fixed times for work, but took it up when it pleased his fancy. His books lay all about him in confusion; he had not a large library - some thousand volumes - and he was fond of pulling out leaves which he thought otiose. Sometimes, if the fancy took him, he would call on a neighbour; when he came home he would play his organ or sing to himself. Then he would go to his books again, and, before his eye sight failed, would read or write; smoke a pipe, and go to bed."

After his sight began to go, he paid a local boy read to him of an evening. Benson writes: "Here he sits, in a dry month, old and blind, being read to by a country boy, longing for rain" which T S Eliot turned into: "Here I am, an old man in a dry month/ Being read to by a boy, waiting for rain" (Benson has the edge, I think). He sat by the fire place in a dressing gown, slippered feet on the fender, wearing a top hat (from which he occasionally took a red silk handkerchief), snuff box in his hand, stroking his beard with a paper-knife. Tennyson visited, with his son, in 1876. Thinking he'd be uncomfortable in the old farmhouse FitzGerald put them in the Bull in the market square opposite the Shire Hall. They hadn't met for twenty years but he still told Tennyson he should have stopped writing thirty-four years ago when he ceased to be a poet and became an artist. Tennyson, in return, wrote an affectionate poem about him as he sat under the apple tree in his garden.

Things were closing in on him now. In 1879, his brother John died. What was left of their father's estates in Lancashire and Suffolk were finally sold out of the family. He was almost teetotal, almost a vegetarian (almost because out of courtesy he ate meat in other people's houses). At home he lived on apples, pears, bread, sometimes a turnip, cheese, and milk pudding. Tea was his favourite meal with bread and country butter. He smoked a clay pipe - presumably a long churchwarden - which he broke into pieces after a single use. He loved colours - bright curtains and carpets, butterflies, moths and birds. He kept a multi-coloured mop for years as a kind of sculptural ornament. He loved birdsong (except the nightingale, which should be in bed like everybody else), "church bells, the wind in the trees, rattle of ropes, the sharp hiss of the sea".

He was a tall unkempt man in baggy sailor-blue clothes. In hot weather he carried his shoes on a stick over his shoulder. One woman observed he was proud, but not too proud to carry his boots to the cobblers to be mended. He was not popular with local people who called him soft in the head and dotty. He could also be peevish, pettish, grumpy, intolerant of having his comfort or habits disturbed, tetchy, and even bad-tempered. He could be cutting. The rector once called to ask him why he was never in church. "Sir," said FitzGerald, "you might have conceived that a man has not come to my years without thinking much on those things. I believe you may say that I have reflected on them fully. You need not repeat this visit." Another time he asked the local bookseller to dinner. When the man arrived, FitzGerald turned him from the door. "I saw you yesterday," he wrote next morning, "but I was not fit for company, and felt that I could not be bothered."

He was active to his last day, troubled by bronchitis but pottering in his garden, playing the organ, occasionally putting to sea in other men's boats. His translation of Sophocles's Œdipus came out in 1880 and '81. In 1883 he published his last book - *Readings from Crabbe.* That last summer, 1883, his nieces shared the farmhouse. In a letter dated 12th June he says he was going the next day to visit the latest George Crabbe, the grandson of the poet. He died in bed in his friend's house early in the morning of the 14th. The words on his tomb in Boulge read: "It is He that hath made us, and not we ourselves" - a curious epitaph for a seventy-four year old agnostic.

FitzGerald was a man for small things: vignettes and glimpses, undertones and impressions. Big things like the work of Milton, Browning or Thackeray were too much for him. In music he preferred Handel - simple but grand. He had a strong sense of *lachrymae rerum* - tears for things, the sadness of things, "the endless pathos of the world." His delight in small things and their pathos - the glance of sunlight on a leaf, caught and then gone - was spoiled by knowing it couldn't last. He was unwilling to suffer, Benson believed, and so couldn't write great poetry - except once, in *The Rubaiyat* when he faced up to the darkness below life. He read, Benson said, to deaden pain.

Benson also claimed he had the insight for lyrical poetry but not the words. If he didn't write nature poetry, the makings of it are certainly in his letters. One June in a letter to Cowell he describes the greenness outside his bedroom window, the scent of hay, the sound of whetstone on scythe, and the roses already passing away. His feeling for things was deep. Here are three quotations from letters to friends, the first in 1842:

> I get radishes to eat for breakfast of a morning: with them comes a savour of earth that brings all the delicious gardens of the world back into one's soul, and almost draws tears from my eyes.

> The trees murmur a continuous soft chorus to the solo which my soul discourses in.

> There's no sea like the Aldburgh Sea. It talks to me.

In reality, it's hard to imagine him far from rustic Suffolk, irritated by the clock in Woodbridge church tower playing "Oh, where is my soldier laddie gone?" every fifteen minutes of every slow country day.

CHAPTER IV

The Scholar-Gipsy

Not many would call Matthew Arnold's *The Scholar-Gipsy* major or *Hamlet* minor but the poem has something of immense value which the play lacks - undertones of eternity, Masefieldian fragments, which, if read while young, will last until they illuminate old age. Arnold does this both through poetry and a portrayal of a landscape, which is enhanced by going there in person: a Platonism of poetry and place side by side.

Arnold found the story of the Scholar-Gipsy, which is apparently true, in Joseph Glanvil's *The Vanity of Dogmatising* (1661). A student of Oxford, too poor to pay his way, joins a band of gypsies to learn how to control other people's minds. Arnold soon forgets this, however, and the scholar-turned-gypsy becomes a listless wanderer on the Cumnor Hills and Berkshire Downs, passively waiting for a "spark from heaven":

> But when the fields are still,
> And the tired men and dogs all gone to rest,
> And only the white sheep are sometimes seen
> Cross and recross the strips of moon-blanch'd green,
> Come, shepherd, and again begin the quest!
>
> While to my ear from uplands far away
> The bleating of the folded flocks is borne,

With distant cries of reapers in the corn -
All the live murmur of a summer's day.

And air-swept lindens yield
Their scent, and rustle down their perfumed showers
Of bloom on the grass where I am laid,
And bower me from the August sun with shade;
And the eye travels down to Oxford's towers.

Shepherds had met him on the Hurst in spring;
At some lone alehouse in the Berkshire moors,
On the warm ingle-bench, the smock-frock'd boors
Had found him seated at their entering.

At some lone homestead in the Cumner hills,
Where at her open door the housewife darns,
Thou hast been seen, or hanging on a gate
To watch the threshers in the mossy barns.

… in my boat I lie
Moor'd to the cool bank in the summer-heats,
'Mid wide grass meadows which the sunshine fills,
And watch the warm, green-muffled Cumner hills,
And wonder if thou haunt'st their shy retreats.

Those mysterious undertones which animate the poem also
animate the hills. The Cumnors are just across the Thames from
Oxford. As an undergraduate in the 1840s Arnold often walked
on them with his friend Arthur Clough. In many places in the
world they'd barely register - five miles long, maybe, two and
a half miles wide, five hundred and fifty feet high at the most.
Five slightly higher points could be called peaks - Cumnor Hill,
Hirst Hill (which are in line with each other) and Boar's Hill
which is separated from them by a low saddle or col. Farther
north-west are Beacon and Wytham Hills.

The range is in fact a coral reef laid down in a tropical Jurassic sea a hundred and fifty million years ago. Outwardly - in places - the tops of the hills haven't changed too much since Arnold's day. Reapers in the corn have gone but corn still grows over the curve of the hills, yellow in late summer against the sky. The hedges are now tall with old gnarled trees. Elder, foxglove, guelder rose, morning glory, shepherd's purse and campion are still common, with loosestrife, meadowsweet and bedstraw down by the river. They're an old man's hills, silent save for the noise which ageing brings, easy on the heart with gentle slopes and folds: "fat" sums them up quite well, hard coral hills though in fact they are. There are no rivers, of course, only cress-hidden rills as described by Arnold in his poem.

But otherwise the hills of *The Scholar-Gipsy* are an Arnold-construct. To begin with they are, in reality, too small to spend several lifetimes wandering over as the scholar turned gipsy does in the poem. Arnold also made them more isolated and rural than they are - he cut out two whole villages, for example, along with their inns and churches. Cumnor village had a population of a thousand in his day and still dominates the summit. In turn it's dominated by a solid church with a confident tower on its own hillock. St Michael's is 11th century in origin, 13th in construction. Did Arnold ever go inside? It has a serenity which comes only with time. In the nave you can hear the ticking of the clock in the tower. The last stroke of the hour echoes for a good thirty seconds before fading back into the deepest silence. The walls are so thick that the midday summer sun never reaches the floor but stays on the slope of the sills. You don't need to believe in anything to be enlarged by the mystery of a space which seems to abolish space itself, and time. It insists on nothing, although it feels like a connector between here and the great elsewhere.

The Bear and Ragged Staff is a 14th century inn on the edge of the village, in the right place to serve drovers and wagoners who for centuries toiled up the steep slope from the river ferry at Bablock Hythe.

The etymology of Cumnor is unknown: "Cuma's hillside", possibly, after an 8th century Abbot of Abingdon. The abbey owned the hills for centuries and in the 14th the monks built a big house called Cumnor Place as the abbot's summer residence (the Thames valley was notoriously sultry in summertime). After the Dissolution of the Monasteries the first secular owner was the last abbot. A few years later, Amy Dudley, wife of the Queen's favourite and future Earl of Leicester, was a tenant. In 1560 she was found dead at the foot of the stairs. Foul play? The authorities said not. The villagers thought otherwise: Amy's ghost haunted the hills for centuries until no fewer than nine Oxford vicars drowned her in the village pond which hasn't frozen over from that day to this. The story's told in Scott's *Kenilworth*. Cumnor's also the Lumsdon of Hardy's *Jude the Obscure*.

By Arnold's time seven thousand acres of the hills belonged to the Earls of Abingdon. In 1814, the 5th Earl, still in his mid-twenties, enclosed the land thereabouts thus creating the landscape in which Arnold placed the Scholar Gipsy who'd begun his wanderings on unenclosed hills a hundred and fifty years earlier. The Earl lived in Wytham House (renamed Abbey in 1850 for no known reason) at the foot of the escarpment at the western end of the range. Arnold razed that as well.

Arnold's at his most graphic in describing the river and the plain fringing the hills. The scenery around Bablock Hythe in particular won't have changed too much, though *The Ferry Boat Inn* is a new building with an unchanged name. A bell for calling the ferryman is still nailed to a willow. Today's ferry, like the old, is essentially a broad beamed punt. Back then, the ferryman hauled on an overhead rope made fast to either bank. Arnold has the Scholar Gipsy reclining in the ferry, trailing his hand in the water. This is unlikely: the gunwale was only a few inches high and the crossing couldn't have taken more than three or four minutes (the river really is a stripling here as Arnold says).

The mill on the Seacourt Stream was also unmissable, although missed out from the poem too. For a couple of miles, this little river flows very rapidly across the Wytham Flats parallel to the Thames. A leat leads out of the stream into the mill and back to the river in a loop. The mill and the miller's house stand on either side while the water wheel would have turned in between them. A stone bridge spans it, joining two great wooden barns which are now, like the house and mill, abandoned (or at least they were when I was last there, now some years ago). Self-sewn willows grow everywhere in the damp soil.

Arnold also eradicated Wytham, a winding village of Oxfordshire stone and thatch. The inn, the *White Hart*, probably has connections to Richard II whose badge it was. There's a dove cote, now birdless, but presumably alive in Arnold's day. The village, and the woods and hills behind, are now owned by the University and so are a bit lifeless and time-stopped but over the centuries the parish register records sawyers and millers, shoemakers and cowmen, shepherds and grooms, hurdle makers, butlers and coachmen (in the big house). In other words, the hills were more dynamic than Arnold allowed.

All Saints in Wytham at first sight looks Tudor with a stumpy tower not much higher than the roof, and a bright blue clock face with golden hands and gilded Roman numerals. It was built, in fact, in 1811 by the 26-year old 5th Earl to replace a ruinous church on the same spot. Partly it was built with material from the old church, partly of stones from Cumnor Place, which also sent down some stained glass. The faces in this glass are pure Queen Anne. Other figures in other windows are distinctively Victorian. Under the belfry is a grey painted gallery with a bright Royal Coat of Arms. The clock chimes tinnily. It's a thoroughly homely little place. Did Arnold stand there in the silence and look at the corbels with the faces of a nun, a bagpiper, a playing-card king, a man in a mitre? The man in the mitre might even be the young Earl himself (he was still alive, then in his sixties, when Arnold passed that way.) The hedge around the churchyard is draped in ivy and the grave stones are lichened into unreadability.

Godstow bridge and lasher - a dialect word for a weir and its pool - appear in the same stanza in the poem, though it's unclear how they're related geographically. To start with, the lasher by the bridge is downstream, not upstream as in the poem. On the right bank stand the ruins of Godstow Abbey. On the left is the *Trout Inn*, again unmentioned although it's prominent and in those days must still have served the rivermen working the upper reaches of the Thames. Here, the river is split by an island, one half pouring over the weir, the other flowing smoothly by on the other side. From down here, too, you can see how exactly right is Arnold's line about "the warm, green-muffled Cumner Hills". (The spelling has changed.)

Sir Arthur Evans, the archaeologist who uncovered Knossos, lived on Boar's Hill in the 1920s and '30s. Nearby he built the Jarn Mound as a monument to the poet and the poem but also to open up a better view of Oxford down on the plain, and to give work to unemployed men in the Slump. The Mound is about fifty feet high. Concrete steps and an iron hand rail get you to the top but a forest of trees now blocks the view of Oxford in the valley and also hide, in the opposite direction, the Vale of the White Horse where Chesterton mistakenly thought the last great battle in the West was fought and won. (The etymology of Jarn is obscure: a corruption of the French *le jardin* is one suggestion.)

John Masefield also lived on Boar's Hill with his bees, goats and garden theatre: Robert Graves visited him when he was up at Oxford after the Great War. Robert Bridges shared the hill for a little while - two Poet Laureates on a few acres of high ground. It was here that Bridges, one of the last Platonists of the old school, wrote *The Testament of Beauty*, to put across Plato's vision, thought and ideas (two sections paraphrase *The Phaedrus*, the book which records the voice of summer by the river).

Today Boar's Hill is densely wooded, dotted everywhere with hidden houses down short driveways. For the elderly it's like stepping back in time, particularly walking down the lane, with guelder roses by the wayside, to Wooton on the plain.

CHAPTER V

Plays and Platonism

The word theatre comes from the Greeks. It means the seeing place. It is the place people come to see the truth about life and the social situation. The theatre is a spiritual and social X-ray of its time. The theatre was created to tell people the truth about life and the social situation.

STELLA ADLER

I regard the theatre as the greatest of all art forms, the most immediate way in which a human being can share with another the sense of what it is to be a human being.

OSCAR WILDE

Art matches the twin wings of Platonism - earth and eternity, learning and untutored light, Being and Becoming. The earthly again divides into two - the Platonic and the non-Platonic, epitomised here by Shakespeare and Ibsen. (Non-Platonic art dominates the West today but like most aspects of modern Western life its roots are 19th century.)

Art at its highest should re-connect us to infinity by stopping thought and creating undertones while the more earthly art teaches us about our own natures, what it is to be human, though mostly the bad bits. Even at the lower level, novels can take you to places which are otherwise out of reach: they can be plotless and one-dimensional yet still expand consciousness: C S Forester's Hornblower stories recruits the reader into the Nelsonic Royal Navy: its techniques, tactics, technology, technicalities, what happened on the orlop deck and how to fire a broadside.

At the highest level, however, fiction can hand us ready-made us insights into the psychology of a species which, to some, would otherwise be inexplicable. Harold Bloom* even claimed that Shakespeare created modern mankind by deepening self-awareness and self-knowledge - and did so in only twelve years, 1594 to 1606, from *King John* to *Antony and Cleopatra*. In *Shakespeare: the Invention of the Human* (1999) Bloom speculates that some time in the latter part of the 16th century the young Shakespeare* must have become aware - suddenly or gradually - that people have (or he himself had) a developable inner world, an evolvable inner life, a consciousness which can expand. The mind is not only expandable, not only complex, but is also filled with contradictory feelings and thoughts which we can scrutinise, analyse and employ in understanding ourselves and others: the crook and the saint live side by side in the same body.

Shakespeare was still only in his mid-twenties when he wrote *King John* and conjured up Faulconbridge, the first fictional character in history to show our inner lives to ourselves. Character after character went on to do the same: Bottom, Mercutio, Portia, Shylock, Richard II all show an "intensity of being" greater than is needed for a part in a play. Plots aren't needed because these personalities rise above mere action and reveal what's inside them, and therefore inside us also. "They have an interior to journey out from" and so are "greater than their fates".

For Bloom, Hamlet was "the most aware and knowing figure ever conceived ". He was also: "cold, murderous, solipsistic, nihilistic, manipulative", a disunity of opposites - emptiness and fullness - who "veers dizzily between being everything and being nothing". Falstaff is almost equally great. "For Hamlet, the self is an abyss, the chaos of virtual nothingness. For Falstaff the self is everything." The ultimate introvert and extravert, perhaps. Falstaff is a Becoming man, locked forever in the material world: Hamlet could, potentially, have sensed eternity except, Bloom suspected, Shakespeare himself was incomplete. Could Shakespeare sense the invisible behind the visible? "Regretfully, no", said Bloom.

Hamlet, I'd add, can be read as the very first portrayal of modern man, a kind of Post-Modernist before his time, spiritually incomplete, ruined by the Reformation which stripped away a religion rich in ritual and certainty and left him alone with his own mind: he couldn't fill the void and as a result never saw life steadily and saw it whole.

If Shakespeare altered the way we see ourselves, Henrik Ibsen (1828-1906) changed not only Western theatre but the West itself - such is the power of non-Platonic art. Ibsen's plays are full of darkness in a society which twisted people out of shape through a stifling conformity, boredom, spiritual emptiness (a Lutheran failure), respectability, and repression - particularly of women. Ugliness destroys and here we have the ugliness of a society which denies people the freedom to live according to the nature of things, to evolve personally and become fulfilled. Ugliness disconnects the person from the peace which tells us all will be well but also opens the predicable chasm of discontent and cruelty.

Brand (1865) is a fiery Lutheran pastor whose deity is not so much the Trinity as the the fierce Old Testament God - give yourself to Him entirely, obey, and so heal your fragmented soul by becoming what He demands. But God, it turns out, disagrees, demanding no such thing: He kills the pastor with an avalanche. (Brand means fire in Norwegian and Danish, in English too but now only in the form of a burning piece of wood or branded cattle.) In *A Doll's House* (1879), Nora Helmer's husband treats her like a dancing doll until he finds out she once fraudulently borrowed money to save his life but, instead of being pleased and grateful (she's repaid the loan), he's outraged at this affront to bourgeois morality. But Nora, true to herself, walks out on their three children, and him, dramatically slamming the door on stage behind her. In *Ghosts* (1881) the dead Captain Alving's son dies of inherited syphilis and his daughter heads off to a brothel - Mrs Alving's family is rotten through and through in spite of her middle class respectability. *Hedda Gabler* (1890) is set in the heroine's living room - a place where not a lot of living is done: Hedda is unloving and sexually frustrated and, after wreaking havoc throughout the play, shoots herself dead. Whatever the ideals, reality always pulls them down.

Ibsen, like his fellow-Norwegian Edvard Munch, was in at the beginning of Realism and Modernism (still running its course as Post-Modernism) but Jacques Barzun thought he'd knocked away the props essential to a civilised society. In *From Dawn to Decadence** Barzun argues that Ibsen's plays "supported the new thesis that the most admired virtues and revered institutions were obstacles to the good life: marriage, always telling the truth, respect for authority, propriety at all costs. All ideals in the abstract are causes of disaster to individuals and ultimately to society".

CHAPTER VI

Poetry and Platonism

*For some three thousand years, poetry has been understood
to be the rhythmical creation of beauty … Further, there is
a connection, not easy to explain, between the difficulties
imposed by the laws of metre and rhyme and the beauty of
the poem.*

*We wish to connect our two worlds, for we cannot be content
to keep them separate.*

*When we try to make the spiritual world real to ourselves,
our natural and inevitable language is the language of
poetry, symbol and myth.*

DEAN INGE

All great Art is Praise.

*Art is not a study of positive reality, it is the seeking for
ideal truth.*

JOHN RUSKIN

Poetry at its best is always Platonist but it's also very rare.
Essentially it's the Way of Beauty that instantly reconnects the

soul to where it comes from. Poetry, said Housman, is to harmonise the sadness of the universe. It's a mix of beauty, balance, harmony, melody, sadness, stillness. Poetry makes a cosmos out of chaos, a place at peace with eternity because its own inner harmony matches that of infinity itself. Stillness, like beauty, is an attribute of eternity and so reconnects. Sadness, too, is natural to a people exiled from their home and surrounded by the loneliness and passingness of things.

Tennyson, for example, presented a harmony of words, metrically ordered, which complete a circuit in the reader who is then instantly plugged into the eternal. The verse's wavelength matches the wavelength of eternity. The rightness of the words matches the rightness of Reality and both are revealed as beauty:

> So all day long the noise of battle rolled
> Among the mountains by the winter sea,
> Until King Arthur's table, man by man,
> Had fallen in Lyonesse about their lord.

And then the Apple Isle of Avalon, which is a line of poetry in its own right:

> Where falls not hail, or rain, or any snow,
> Nor ever wind blows loudly: but it lies
> Deep-meadowed, happy, fair with orchard lawns
> And bowery hollows crowned with summer sea,
> Where I will heal me of my grievous wound.

Oddly enough it was often the lesser poets who produced a few lines (nobody produces many) of the real thing. Three years before the Great War, John Masefield wrote *The Everlasting Mercy*, a long poem about redemption through mysticism. Saul

Kane is a poacher, seducer, drunk, liar, and all round wastrel until an old Quaker lady triggers an experience of eternity:

> The station brook, to my new eyes,
> Was babbling out of Paradise.

Masefield also understood how Arnoldian culture works: Homer, for example, lives on in the mind to make life fuller and better: fallen Troy becomes "a city in the soul". What he called "fragments" also appear in his work - intimations of immortality, undertones of the unseen, spots of time, which stay in the mind and illuminate life forever. Understandably, his fragments are most often those of a Victorian boyhood - buccaneers on the Spanish Main, hornpipes and pirates, pieces of eight and bottles of rum. Often too there's a tinge of melancholic stillness about them. First came the good times, the days of yore when carefree sailormen danced barefoot on sun-hot decks or the sanded floors of taverns by tropical seas:

> With the silver seas around us
> and the pale moon overhead.
> And the look-out not a-looking
> and his pipe-bowl glowing red.

Then the grey-souled Board of Trade took the colour out of life, though leaving the undertones or fragments behind to make the spirit less mean and spiteful:

> The schooners and the merry crews are laid away to rest
> A little south the sunset in the Islands of the Blest.

Poetry is a balance between what is said and how it's said, between form and content. It can convey beauty in both these ways - content can even include ideas*, an unfashionable concept these days: when Yeats spoke about ideas in poetry to the members of the Rhymers' Club, in Fleet Street's *Cheshire Cheese*, "a gloomy silence fell on the room". One unnamed young Irish poet accused him of talking like a man of letters. The other Rhymers were more polite - mostly Oxbridge men - but they probably agreed. Yet the West has a long tradition of poetry about ideas and insights, even work. Arnold's *Empedocles on Etna** is a curious mix of wrong and right ideas out of which a workable philosophy of life can be extracted.

Poetry is also a pattern, a harmony, of sound based on a language's deepest characteristic. English is a heavily stressed language, the basis of its poetry: take care of the stressed syllables and the unstressed can take care of themselves, that's all that Hopkins meant by Sprung Rhythm. Master *Bo Peep* or *Jack and Jill* and you've mastered English prosody. It's always been that way - which tells us just how fundamental it is.

From the Old English *Deor*:

Thaes ofereode thisses swa maeg
(That passed so may this).

From William Langland's *Piers Plowman*:

In a summer season when soft was the sun.

The 14th century *Piers Plowman* is a late example of alliterative verse, the universal poetic form of Old English which was, of course, still inflected and so not right for i. Even so, rhyme did appear at least by the 9th century. This is from *Judith*, the only poem in Old English with a woman as hero:

wyrmum bewunden witum gebunden
(in worms wound in torment bound).

Rhyme is the final harmoniser. As Wilde said there's something intrinsically spiritual or eternal about it. It chimes with something fundamental, an echo of eternity. Chaucer perfected it in the clarity of the new hybrid Middle English of the 14th century:

And specially, from every shires ende
Of Engelond, to Caunturbury they wende.

English in fact is now a hybrid of five languages: Greek, Latin, French, Old Norse and Old English. On the whole - though it's no universal rule - ON and OE words are usually better for poetry: shorter, sharper, often carrying the meaning in the sound - slip, slap, sneer, click, clack, grind, grit, grate, greet, creak, croak, crake, crackle. And hiss, a word which also hisses (but then so does sibilance but with a subtle difference) - the language in fact is overloaded with esses and so tends to hiss if words are chosen sloppily. (Ugliness is Old Norse - from *ugga* "to dread" - with the Old English suffix "-ness". It raises the Old Norse caveman-like noise to a more sophisticated level which expresses what it means through the way it sounds.)

Moonlight in art is a better generator of undertones than it is in physical reality perhaps because, when bathed in it, it clings, envelopes and hampers sight, the primary gateway to eternity. However in art - in poetry and painting (less so in music) - it can work. Compared to his tragedies, Shakespeare's *A Midsummer Night's Dream* might seem trifling yet it's also a perfect example of a Masefieldian fragment: even when the details of the plot are forgotten the play illuminates life through memories of moonlight and the moonlit greenwood. Moon imagery dominates the play yet it's mentioned only a dozen times - and only once memorably: "Ill met by moonlight", says Oberon to Titania.

The greenwood is equally dominant:

I know a bank where the wild thyme blows,
Where oxlips and the nodding violet grows,
Quite over-canopied with luscious woodbine,
With sweet musk-roses, and with eglantine.

And sounds:

Yet mark'd I where the bolt of Cupid fell.
It fell upon a little western flower,
Before milk-white, now purple with love's wound,
And maidens call it Love-in-idleness.

There's poetry's in the word "love-in-idleness" which is also called, beautifully, heartsease and yet in fact it's the common pansy, from the French for "thought".

Harmony is also in the baying of the hounds hunting in the woods at daybreak, their voices like a peal of bells in a church belfry, different tones and pitches blending and harmonising, ringing out across the meadows. None of this is described, of course, but the image is implanted in the mind.

The elemental immortals, Oberon and Titania are flawed by the ugliness of ego and therefore of ignorance but they too, along with Puck, add undertones by uncovering another layer of being, one lying between the mortal and the everlasting, rather than the eternal - a layer of extra life, a level of consciousness below the Trinity's but above our own, an everlastingness embedded (somehow) in eternity.

As already said, lesser poets, in fact, write the bulk of those very few poems which directly connect Becoming to Being by contracting the mind through beauty and sadness for things - inadvertently, at times, since not all had a sense of eternity. A E Housman (1859-1936) didn't but he knew all about sorrow:

I, a stranger and afraid
In a world I never made.

He wrote only two very short books of poetry, a quarter of a century apart. The first, *A Shropshire Lad* (1896) is best from the Platonism point of view although it appealed, it used to be said, mainly to adolescent boys. It's largely about landscape and loneliness, Redcoats and exile, gallows and ale. Somehow he captured, if only in a very few of his poems, that essential sense of tears for things, the loneliness at the heart of time and place. Most of the poems are iambic tetrameters, all are short and readable, their meaning understandable at a glance - in other words they engage directly without the need of a crib or the bafflement that comes without one. They're self-harmonious and scan perfectly with very few spondees, or two stressed syllables side by side. His Platonist poems are usually about place - places, I believe, which he'd never visited when he wrote about them: as a boy he lived in Worcestershire from where could see the Clee Hills of Shropshire to the West (the sound of the place names inspired him, it's said).

On the idle hill of summer,
Sleepy with the flow of streams,
Far I hear the steady drummer
Drumming like a noise in dreams.

In summertime on Bredon
The bells they sound so clear;
Round both the shires they ring them

In steeples far and near.

Far in a western brookland
That bred me long ago
The poplars stand and tremble
By pools I used to know.

High the vanes of Shrewsbury gleam
Islanded in Severn stream;
The bridges from the steepled crest
Cross the water east and west.

In Zen there's a *do* - or a way to eternity - for practically everybody: *gado* for the painter, *chado* for the Tea Ceremony, *bushido* for the soldier, *jindo* for the philosopher, *shodo* for the calligrapher, *kendo* and *judo* for fighters. (*Shinto* is the way of the gods.) *Kado* is the way of the poet and haiku is the means. To begin with, brevity is built into them: the *haijin*, or haiku poet, has only seventeen syllables (or *onji*) to work with. Originally they were called hokku which was (still is) the opening verse of a long poem jointly written by different people. Haiku evolved as poems in their own right in the late 17th century, mainly through Bashō (1644-1698), who was (possibly) a samurai by birth, a wandering poet and teacher by choice or necessity. (His pen name means banana plant). To write haiku, he said, you need mystery, tranquillity, simplicity, elegance and grace - the very things they uncover and reveal. Blyth went further: a haiku is a sacrament in its own right. It's spiritual poetry perfected, purpose-made for creating undertones through thought-blocking, and it does so mainly through placing an image from nature alongside a manmade one, set in a season. The best are also perfectly crafted to convey a sense of the loneliness, the fleetingness of things.

The following are paraphrases of Blyth's translations:

Buson:

Evening. The inn roof leaks. A cherry tree droops.
Spring day. Sea rising, falling, all day.

Otsuji

Spring rain. Between the trees, a path to the sea.

Shiki:

Summer rain. Alone in the office.
In the summer heat, white houses by the creek.
Temple gods. Far off, a June sea.
A lonely railway station. Lotus flowers blooming

For poetry of the Platonic kind, brevity is always crucial and in English that often means picking out couplets or short stanzas from longer poems. *Recessional,* written in 1897 for the Queen's Diamond Jubilee, is about the receding of imperial power which Kipling fears will happen, since all things end. Most people shy away from Kipling nowadays but, taken out of context, one couplet lives on as a timeless undertone in its own right:

The tumult and the shouting dies,
The captains and the kings depart.

Why does it work? Perhaps because it can stand alone without a back story but with sadness for the passing of all unnamed, unknown things. It captures a sadness of fleetingness, of passingness.

From Wordsworth also we learn that imagery of some kinds of people can be a gateway to the Beyond - particularly the rugged, the damaged, the solitary, the abandoned, the hurt, the old (who hear eternity calling). Each is like a quiet force of nature. Above all there's the leech-gatherer. A traveller is crossing a high moor on a bright morning after a night of storm. (There's a nice snapshot of a hare carrying a glittering mist of water around her paws as she races in the sun.) The traveller meets an old man who makes his living collecting leeches from ponds and selling them, presumably, to doctors:

> From pond to pond he roamed, from moor to moor;
> Housing, with God's good help, by choice or chance;
> And in this way he gained an honest maintenance.

If, at a higher level, people are both human and divine, at a lower one they're both human and elemental. The leech-gatherer is a bit of the landscape - not *like* a bit of the landscape, but an actual part of it, like a rock left behind by an ice sheet. (In the poem, Wordsworth likens him to a beast which has crawled out of the sea.) He's a man simplified almost to the inorganic, yet at the same time he has courtesy, grace, and gentleness. He's bent double with age and hardship after a rough life in wild places, and yet he's well-spoken:

> Choice word and measured phrase, above the reach
> Of ordinary men; a stately speech.

Paradoxically the beauty of speech can work even if it's about a dark and meaningless world. This is from Thomson's *The City of Dreadful Night*. The tears here are not for the loneliness of things but for people cut off from beauty and eternity through a damaged psychology or inadequacy:

This little life is all we must endure,
The grave's most holy place is ever sure,
We fall asleep and never wake again.

O Brothers of sad lives! they are so brief;
A few short years must bring us all relief
In all eternity I had one chance,
One few years' term of gracious human life:
The splendours of the intellect's advance,
The sweetness of the home with babes and wife;
My wine of life is poison mixed with gall,
My noonday passes in a nightmare dream.

My Brother, my poor Brothers, it is thus,
This life holds nothing good for us
But it ends soon and never more can be.
I ponder these thoughts and they comfort me.

How important is meaning in poetry? Eliot said that looking
for it is useful in distracting the mind while the real meaning of
the poem slips into the sub-conscious. For Eliot, that real meaning
seems to have been an under-layer of emotion, outside the reach of
the intellect, and which can in some cases last lifelong - and what
Masefield called a fragment and I've been calling an undertone.
The problem here, it seems to me, is that when confronted with a
puzzle, the mind usually won't rest until it's solved - and infinity is
encountered only by the shut down mind. Yet the difficult to understand can work: in Shakespeare's *Troilus and Cressida* Ulysses says:

Time hath, my lord, a wallet at his back,
Wherein he puts alms for oblivion.

What this means isn't obvious at first and it turns out to say,
simply, that the good is soon forgotten but there's a sadness in

the wording as well as a vaguer sense of the loneliness of time. On top of that, the phrase - alms for oblivion - is memorable, an undertone in sound alone.

Yeats's *Sailing to Byzantium* is another example - like "alms for oblivion" it goes against the general rule about clarity and understandability. It's so obscure it's best read with a crib, although none of the crib-writers explain the hardest bits. W B Yeats (1865-1939) wrote it in his early sixties, hardly ancient these days but it can be taken as an old man's thoughts turning to eternity and away from the swarming sensual life on earth, so busy with getting, begetting, and dying that "monuments to unageing intellect" are neglected:

> And therefore I have sailed the seas and come
> To the holy city of Byzantium.

Knowing the poet's thoughts also helps. If he could spend one month in the distant past, Yeats wrote, Byzantium would be the place. "I think I could find in some little wine-shop some philosophical worker in mosaic who would answer all my questions, the supernatural descending nearer to him than to Plotinus even." He saw it as city of narrow streets filled with wine shops, goldsmiths, and workers in enamel where heaven was close to earth.

CHAPTER VII

Plato in Pictures

One purpose of art is to open a way for people to sense the invisible beyond the visible, the unseen through the seen. That being so you'd expect painting to be most effective although I suspect music, particularly classical, comes first, followed by poetry, the portable Plato.

Photographs, oddly enough (they seem so mechanical) can work better than many a painting. Tight shots are best - you can take them in at a glance and they're something the naked eye can't really pick out unaided. A mobile phone will do - you don't need a DSLR or mirrorless camera, or photoshop. Sunlight is doubly important - a sunless scene may work in the physical world but not in a photograph.

Ansel Adams (1902-1984) might have agreed: "When I'm ready to make a photograph," he tells us in a documentary about his work, "I think I see in my mind's eye something that is not literally there". He worked in black and white, long before the digital age, in the wilderness of what is now the Yosemite National Park in California where everything is on a gigantic scale - groves of sequoia, barely scaleable granite crags, rock peak beyond rock peak, each thousands of feet high. A landscape, in fact, more like Burke's Sublime than the Beautiful yet, in his developed photographs, Adams conveyed a sense of something greater than the merely physical, however great that is. Emerson and Edward Carpenter (1844-1929) influenced him, I believe. In turn, Whitman and Hinduism influenced Carpenter's long prose-poem, *Towards Democracy* - the world will be democratic when everybody experiences cosmic consciousness, or eternity.

Platonist painting began in the 15th century Italian Renaissance when many people were more naturally attuned to whatever's beyond physical reality. The new art, therefore, resonated and elevated them more easily than it can today. Sandro Botticelli (1445-1510), for example, painted *The Birth of Venus* some time around 1484, the year when Ficino completed his translations of Plato and Plotinus. Possibly - probably - it was a consciously Neo-Platonic creation. From today's point of view we can make the case that Aphrodite has just risen from the sea, the familiar story of a god-incarnate, riding a sea shell as two lesser deities, the wind and the breeze, waft her ashore where the goddess of the Spring welcomes with her a cloak to cover her nakedness, divinity being too overwhelming for direct sight. Portrayed here is rebirth, renewal, renaissance, the old re-found, an entire civilisation about to spring to life again. Aphrodite symbolises eternity rising into the world of common day. She ticks the checklist - the unseen in the seen, eternal peace in her stance, sadness for our mortality, serenity in her face, eyes looking wistfully back from whence she came. But she is also the symbol of the West's origin in Antiquity, a lesson about the Hellenic origins of our civilisation.

Some four hundred years later, Zen rather than Plato influenced Claude Monet (1840-1926). Later in life Monet lived in Giverny, in Normandy, on the banks of the Seine fifty or so miles north of Paris. He diverted the River Epte to make a pond which he planted with water lilies, the nearest he could get to the Eastern lotus. For some thirty years, beginning in 1889, he painted that pond, and its reflections of willow, cloud and sky, around two hundred and fifty times. In 1914, now with badly cataract-damaged eyes, he began painting the eight great curved panels, showing the light on the water from dawn to dusk, which are now in the Musée de l'Orangerie in Paris. "These are not paintings," he said of them, "they are objects of contemplation". They may work as aids to introvertive meditation but they miss that true extrovertive spontaneity although at least one, showing the Japanese bridge and not just the water's surface, does offer glimpses of something unseeable and greater.

Monet was also in at the beginning of Impressionism, an intensely Gallic affair. The name, in fact, came from the title of his painting of the harbour at Le Havre, *Impression, Sunrise,* first shown to the public in 1874, exactly four hundred years after Ficino finished his translations. New technologies both pushed and pulled the Impressionists. Photography, which mechanically copies what the physical eye sees, pushed them into doing things differently. At the same time, small tubes of portable paint came on the market, letting artists to work out of doors and in theatres, bars and boulevards. They were fresh colours, too - cadmium yellow, ultramarine blue, cobalt blue - with a new vibrancy.

Modern landscape painting, Wilde writes in *De Profundis,* showed a "subtlety and sensitiveness of impression, its suggestion of a spirit dwelling in external things and making its raiments of earth and air, of mist and city alike … Far off, like a pearl, one can see the City of God. It is so wonderful that it seems as if a child could reach it in a summer's day." Barzun argued that Impressionism was Romanticism's last stand, culminating in a philosophy of light. "It is light and colour and colour and light that defines Romanticism in paint." And again: "The Impressionist painters worked on the principle that the play of light was the true reality; objects are not solid things with a definite outline and colour that we take them to be." They used a technique called optical merging: if you put two pure colours close together they'll look brighter and more luminous than if physically mixed.

As a general rule, their landscapes work better than their absinthe drinkers, barmaids and ballet dancers and we can take

Monet's *La Pie* (The Magpie) (1868/9) almost as a random example. A solitary magpie perches on a rickety gate in a wattle fence in front of snow covered trees, and a farmhouse roof: the fields beyond are as white with snow as is the sky with light, making a world that is almost horizonless and boundary-free. The footpath leading to the gate is strangely more brightly lit, almost luminous, leading to something less earthly. Here is the seen letting in the unseen.

On the other hand, Paul Gauguin (1848-1903) claimed that the Impressionists merely painted what the eye can see, not the inner mystery. In the 1880s, he became a Symbolist or what he called a Synthetist. Mallarmé summed up Symbolist painting: "peindre non la chose, l'effet qu'elle produit." "Don't paint the thing, paint the effect it has on you." In the 1890s, Gauguin was in Tahiti painting what to Europeans was still a very far away place, vivid with tropical colour. By now he was saying: "The essence is what is not expressed".

Modernism, Platonism's antithesis, began in 1893 with Munch's *Scream*. Quite a debut, but the painter says nothing deep about life or eternity, only about his own shortcomings and a society that had lost its way: art reflecting corrosion but unable to create anything to counteract it. Expressionism began in Germany in 1905, in what was once called the long Edwardian summer, yet it too displayed disturbed minds and a damaged society. Picasso painted *Les Demoiselles d'Avignon* two years later. If the human world is empty, broken and in pieces, then the artist should paint it that way: the form should be broken as well as the content. "Show, not tell." As for Dali's Post-War Surrealism - if there's no objective truth, then paint the world as hallucination. Spengler, writing in 1918, said the newly established avant-garde was turning against its own society and tearing it apart.

Yet Modernism modified by mysticism can at least half-work as we see in Paul Nash, a lesser late Victorian painter, born 1889, whose landscape and war paintings were influenced, first, by Blake and Palmer (two extremely mystical painters) and secondly by the very unmystical Continentals - Picasso, Cocteau, Ernst, Magritte. Nash admired the "real mental daring" of the French as opposed to British "safety first". Yet Nash was probably one of those artists who Inge said were close to eternity without directly sensing it. He was essentially a landscape artist and his more home-grown paintings can still reveal what he called "the things behind".

From 1912 Nash several times painted Wittenham Clumps, across the Thames from Dorchester in Oxfordshire. In 1911 he wrote to a friend, Mercia Oakley: "The country about and about is marvellous - Grey hollowed hills crowned by old old trees, Pan-ish places down by the river wonderful to think on, full of strange enchantment ... a beautiful legendary country haunted by old gods long forgotten." Although he painted only one clump, there are in fact two - Round and Castle Hills. His best paintings are close-ups which highlight the small wood on the summit. (The woods are still there, a bit bigger now than in Nash's day.)

Time - what Plato called "the moving image of eternity" - can also induce that sense of the invisible. Castle Hill is topped by an Iron Age fort with ingeniously engineered ramparts and ditches, the biggest ones facing the Berkshire Downs on the summits of which lived rival tribes. Farmers from the Bronze Age to the Roman period lived on the flanks of Round Hill for well over fifteen centuries - with a three hundred year Iron Age gap during which, so archaeologists surmise, people lived on the plain and farmed the hill from below.

Nash was also at the end of a long line of English pre-Modernist landscape watercolourists - John Sell Cotman (1782-1842), for example, and Francis Towne (1739/40-1816) whose work also give glimpses of "the things behind". Cotman is at his best with sunlight on old buildings - a granary, an inn by a river, a half-tumbled down but still lived in rustic cottage - and pencil sketches of Norfolk churches and Norman doorways. There's the necessary sadness in the sunlight on Chirk Aqueduct in North Wales, the arches reflected in the river. Francis Towne also painted sunlight and, more unusually, he outlined landscapes in black ink. He's at his best with mountains and hill country - Rydal Water in Westmorland or sheer sided rocks in Italy - often in pale blue and a kind of golden brown, all redolent of sunlight, sadness and rest.

If Nash were at the lesser end of the Platonic spectrum, Samuel Palmer* (1805-1881) was at the greater and, unusually, was articulate about it. As with Wordsworth, his instinct for the invisible lasted for only about ten years, while he was still in his twenties and early thirties. Where Wordsworth found an Eden in the Quantock Hills and Ambleside, Palmer found his in Kent - which at one time was, in fact, called the Garden of England. From the mid-1820s he lived in a painters' colony in Shoreham in the Darent valley. He called the place *The Valley of Vision* and the painters called themselves *The Ancients*, because the old ways were better. He painted a different kind of Platonism* - moonlight on a deeply rural landscape and richly blossomed orchards and corn fields.

Palmer revered Blake so much that it's said he kissed the old man's door bell (or threshold, accounts vary) whenever he visited. In particular Blake's wood-cuts illustrating Virgil's *Eclogues* overwhelmed him. In them (to re-arrange his own words slightly) he saw "the mystic glimmer which penetrates and kindles the inmost soul and gives complete delight unlike the gaudy sunlight of the world". In a letter he said he'd put up with anything so long as he could sometimes "look over the doors of bliss".

In a Shoreham Garden and *The Magic Apple Tree* are his two most famous paintings. They combine a fairly obvious symbolism of Eden and apples - one tree growing in a walled garden, the other in a tightly enclosed valley - with a wholly unique style of painting which owed a little to Turner and Blake but more to his own instinct.

In a Shoreham Garden, a watercolour, is now in the Victoria and Albert Museum in London. It's quite small - around twelve inches high. Palmer painted it when he was twenty-four in 1829. It's like the garden of Eden without the snake but dominated by an apple tree in full Maytime blossom: summer is ahead, Autumn far away, the apples are uneaten and we are unfallen. A lady in a red and white dress with a trailing hem stands, small in the distance, at the end of a path at the end of a tunnel of trees. She's too far away to see her face but she's looking up - at what? She herself, in fact, is like the pupil in an eye.

The Magic Apple Tree, about thirteen inches high, is in the Fitzwilliam Museum in Cambridge. The catalogue calls it a "Pen and Indian ink, watercolour, in places mixed with a gum-like medium." Palmer painted it in 1830 when he was twenty-five. Again it's an arched picture: fully leafed trees arch over a curve of hills which are bright yellow with corn, some already reaped and sheaved or stooked. In the foreground a shepherdess plays a pipe while her flock of very wooly sheep rest or sleep. Abundance almost absorbs a grey church steeple. A tree, every bough bent by an impossible harvest of round red apples, leans over a rural lane.

In 1835 with two fellow Ancients, Edward Calvert and Henry Walter, Palmer took a steamer around the coast from London to North Wales where he painted half a dozen water-falls. In *The Black Waterfall, near Dolgelly* (Dolgellau), the river pours down in two stages through a ravine arched, once again, by delicate birch trees. There's an unworldly or other-worldly blueness about the picture: the water is blue-tinged and some of the rocks and the bark of the silver birches are blue. The eye however doesn't fall with the river: it rises to a gap in the trees, then into eternity beyond.

Palmer was also aware of the sadness of things and the still-ness which comes with it. In June, 1836, he was again in Wales and wrote: "Blessed thoughts and visions haunt the Stillness and the twilight of the Soul: and one of the great arts of life is the manufacturing of this stillness." Yet around this time his insight seems to have left him, taking his ability as a painter with it though in his seventies something like the old way of seeing may have returned - unusual as that would be - and which he caught in at least one etching, the art form of his old age.

In their last few years Palmer and his wife lived first in Reigate and then in Redhill where he had his own small studio, barred to all but himself, with a patch of soil for his own wild flowers. The rest of the house and garden, Mrs Palmer's domain, were tidy, dust-free and regimented. He also began a new career as an etcher. Some etchings were for his own translation of Virgil's *Eclogues* but Ruskin's solicitor, Leonard Valpy, who paid little and tried to pay less, also hired him to illustrate Milton's *L'Allegro* and *Il Penseroso*:

> Or let my lamp at midnight hour
> Be seen in some high lonely tower
> Where I may oft outwatch the Bear
> With thrice-great Hermes, or unsphere
> The spirit of Plato to unfold
> What worlds or what vast regions hold
> The immortal mind that hath forsook
> Her mansion in this fleshly nook.

Aristotle distinguished between black and golden melancholy (Robert Burton does something similar in *The Anatomy of Melancholy* (1621)). This poem is about the golden kind which can lead *un penseroso*, or thoughtful man, to mystic union with the divine. In Palmer's etching there's a light in *The Lonely Tower* and a big sickle moon lying on her back on the far horizon, brightening part of the sky, shining on a flock of sheep and two shepherds as well as streaks of cloud. It also shines on the trunks of a clump of trees whose foliage leans over and, in turn, seem to shade the moon, just like the arched landscapes of his younger days. A wagon strains up the shaded side of the hill. The tower may have been based on a real one near Lynmouth in Devon.

On the other hand, there was (still is) a tower on Leith Hill, the highest point of the Surrey range which in those days was treeless. (The tower was built to raise the hills to a thousand feet, the definition of a mountain back then.) As the old man etched his copper plates, a young Ralph Vaughan Williams, a fellow mystic who never lost his sense of eternity, was growing up in the big house below the lonely tower on the slopes of Leith Hill.

CHAPTER VIII

Music's Magic Casement

Ralph Vaughan Williams* (1872-1958) was a lifelong mystic. As early as 1903, when he was twenty one, he quoted Carlyle: "If we search deep enough there is music everywhere." In 1920, when he was forty-eight, he said art exists to reveal the spiritual to which the senses are blind. In 1932, aged sixty, he said: "The object of art is to stretch out to the ultimate realities through the medium of beauty". Music, he said in 1942, when he was seventy, was a "spiritual experience": after the War, people would have to turn back to the eternal. Even in his eighties he could fall into a silence bordering on trance over the beauty of a sunset. In 1958, aged eighty-six, he wrote to the children in a primary school in Swaffham in Norfolk. Music, he told them, lets you see the essence of things in a way science can't: the arts open "magic casements" through which to see what lies beyond.

Natural noises don't have the same impact as sights - apart perhaps for bird song in the Spring - yet, paradoxically organised noise - music - is the best manmade way of reaching the Immaterial. All the same, music which can open the casement is still, in fact, rare. What enables it to evoke eternity is a mystery though I suspect that melody - a linear succession of single notes obeying the rules of its key - is the main cause and connector. Simplicity and brevity, too, is essential. Vaughan Williams wrote at least three such pieces: *The Lark Ascending, Fantasia on Greensleeves*, and most especially *The Fantasia on a Theme of Thomas Tallis*.

Two of these tunes are Tudor and are, of course, fantasias - variations on a theme. His *Greensleeves* is pretty much the unadorned and unaltered 16th century tune. The adaptation began as incidental music for *The Merry Wives of Windsor* in 1912. (Falstaff says: "Let the sky rain potatoes, let it thunder to the tune of *Greensleeves*".) In its own day *Greensleeves* was a hymn, a dance tune, and the lament of a man deserted by his lover who, possibly, is also a prostitute (green carried that meaning). The traditional words are also simple and moving, catching exactly the feeling of sadness that lies at the heart of life, and the loneliness of things:

> Alas, my love, you do me wrong
> To cast me off discourteously
> For I have loved you well and long,
> Delighting in your company.
> Greensleeves was all my joy,
> Greensleeves was my delight,
> Greensleeves was my heart of gold,
> And who but my Lady Greensleeves?

The Lark Ascending seems strangely modern in a 21st century when nobody could possibly write anything like it. It was also unfashionable when first performed in 1920 - the era of Edith Sitwell's *Façade* and the Bright Young Things. In fact Vaughan Williams started to write it pre-Great War for the violinist Marie Hall. It accurately turns into music the words of a poem by another Victorian mystic, George Meredith (1828-1909). The poem is a short-long one, a hundred and twenty odd lines, matched almost exactly by the music at around fifteen minutes. In *An Oxford Elegy* (his setting of Arnold's *The Scholar Gipsy*) the music is inferior to the poetry: here it's superior. The lark

... rises and begins to round,
He drops the silver chain of sound,
Of many links without a break,
In chirrup, whistle, slur and shake.
For singing 'til his heaven fills,
'Tis love of earth that he instils,
And ever winging up and up,
Our valley is his golden cup,
And he the wine which overflows
To lift us with him as he goes:
The woods and brooks, the sheep and kine
He is, the hills, the human line,
The meadows green, the fallow brown.

What is missing from *An Oxford Elegy* is all here: a pastoral portrayal. The valley like a golden cup could be a dip in the Cumnor Hills filled with ripening corn although the composer probably had the high chalk plains of Wiltshire in mind. The last three lines show us the oneness below all things - the lark *is* the river and the sheep, the poet and the composer.

The *Tallis* suite was written to be played in Gloucester Cathedral, part of the 1910 Three Choirs Festival. Vaughan Williams had been asked to write it so it was composed with the acoustics of a medieval cathedral in mind. It's based on a hymn written in the Phrygian mode by Thomas Tallis, organist and composer, for the Archbishop of Canterbury's 1567 *Psalter*. It was composed for religion and then re-composed for a religious place by an atheist with mystic leanings. Holst is said to have walked the streets of the city all night in a daze after hearing it. Not everybody was so enchanted, but the critic from *The Times* wrote: "Throughout its course one is never quite sure whether one is listening to something very old or very new."

Pythagoras in the 6th century BC was the first musicologist - music, he recognised, is mathematically organised noise and its orderliness is a perfect analogy for the cosmos. Unorganised chaos is still there in the silence between the notes. Mathematics, he also realised, is eternal, a human discovery not an invention. Furthermore, music proves the essential goodness of Being.

Music, in other words, illustrates the need to obey the nature of things. Obey and you're connected to Being: disobey and you have jarring disconnecting ugliness.

In Plato's *Republic*, the mystic philosopher-kings are chosen early in childhood and raised amid beauty, devoid of the ugliness which cramps and damages. Music - along with poetry - harmonises and balances their souls to make them whole and complete. In *The Laws*, Plato put the decay of society down to loud music and the wild behaviour of the people who listen to it or, rather, hear it. That, and the fact that they also abuse freedom by letting it all hang out. Nobody respects authority and the most inexpert think they're experts.

Five hundred years after Plato, Plotinus wrote that musicians are more open to beauty than most people: they have a longing for the order which makes the world beautiful. All the same, they must be taught that eternal Beauty is the source of the harmony in the music they make. Melody is eternal, a discovery or a gift. He also thought a single note, a single patch of colour, was enough to make the connection.

It's often said - and perhaps as often disputed - that Minor keys are the vehicles for grief, sorrow, heartbreak. You can read lists of the emotions which individual keys evoke: C Minor - the perils and pain of earthly love: C sharp Minor - grieving and sorrow: G Minor - failure and anxiety, and so on. That said, *The Tallis Suite* is in Major keys and is as sorrowful as you can get. *The Lark Ascending* is also in a Major key and, as the theory says, soaring and full of joy - yet we also hear those strange undertones of sadness somewhere in the notes, or between them.

Edward Elgar (1857-1934) composed the *Enigma Variations* in 1898/99. Each is a musical sketch of a friend or family member. He called them enigmas because he never revealed who they were though, naturally, people have tried to identify them. *Nimrod*, the Mighty Hunter, is August Jaeger (German for hunter). Jaeger worked for the music publisher, Novello, in London and helped Elgar through professional doubts and depression. *Nimrod* is probably the best known of the *Variations* and with a reason. Military bands, for example, play it at the Cenotaph in London on Armistice Day each year: its profound sadness matches the sense of loss of so many men, in so many wars, but particularly in Flanders fields. Yet *Nimrod* also works Platonically although, it has to be said, it in very small parts - only a few seconds in a four minute piece. If the why and the how is unknown, the where isn't and a sung version best illustrates it. Voces8, a cappella octet, sang the words of *Lux Aeterna* (eternal light) set to the *Nimrod* tune on Armistice Day in 2016:

> eternal rest
> give to them, O Lord,
> and let everlasting light shine upon them.

The eternity-evoking passages, which cancel time and let eternity flow through, comes when the soprano reaches her highest notes, in perfect clarity in a few briefs moments of extraordinary power.

Darwin suggested that, before speech evolved, hominids and early humans communicated through wordless sing-song mouth music which express moods, possibly even simple ideas, and warn of danger. Gibbons, apparently, still do. The human sings-song-speakers would, presumably, have expressed feelings of sadness through the three semi-tones of the Minor Third and this has been carried over into language. Research (in 2010) at Tufts University in Massachusetts suggested, possibly, that the

Minor Third is still used in speech - it is, presumably, the Dying
Fall of poetry, as in T S Eliot's *The Love Song of J Alfred Prufrock*:

> For I have known them all already, known them all -
> Have known the evenings, mornings, afternoons,
> I have measured out my life with coffee spoons;
> I know the voices dying with a dying fall
> Beneath the music from a farther room.
> So how should I presume?

CHAPTER IX

Plato, Ruskin and the Welfare State

In politics, he (Ruskin) was a disciple of Plato. He sought to reconstruct society on the Platonic conception of Justice - assigning to each man his due place, and requiring from each man the fulfilment of his duties.

EDWARD TYAS COOK

Ruskin was a Platonist, steeped in the study of Plato, and bound to him by complete sympathy. We cannot separate Ruskin the art-critic from Ruskin the social reformer.

Never since civilisation began has such ugliness been created as the modern English or American town. Ruskin saw in these structures a true index of the mind of their builders and inhabitants, and the sight filled him with horror.

Ruskin could not avert his eyes from the modern town, as Wordsworth did, because the modern town meant a great deal to him, and all of it was intolerable. He observed that the disappearance of beauty in human productions synchronised with the invention of machinery and the development of great industries, and he could not doubt that the two changes were interconnected.

Among other things, John Ruskin (1819-1900) was a Platonist, a mystic, an art and architecture critic, political reformer, writer, artist, geologist, botanist, ecologist, conservationist, Christian (twice over) who read Plato and the Bible every day. Like Plato he wanted to change society: in the long run, Plato changed the world, in the short term Ruskin helped to change the West - particularly society's attitude to the concept of the work-life balance, and the ideas behind the Welfare State.

But Ruskin can also be called one of the world's great Hidden Influencers, one of those radical thinkers whose ideas are taken up by others but which don't seem so revolutionary when the revolution makes them commonplace.

In his day he was a famous art critic who became a political reformer in midlife. The first incarnation was the source of the second. He was quite a good artist, influenced by Turner - landscapes, architecture, botany, rocks, stones, birds, nature - and his politics grew out of discoveries he made in his twenties from his study of paintings and, more particularly, his drawings of nature. Through his sketches* he discovered what he called the Law of Help. As I understand it, he saw the leaves of a tree - for example - as a community of individuals working together for the health and well-being of the whole. Each leaf is similar but not the same: each is individual but designed to cooperate with all the others. Deep universal rules determine the shape of all things, how they look and behave - leaf, flower, tree, painting, poem or piece of music. Variety overlays symmetry, unity underlies diversity, the changeless controls the changing.

A painting, too, is a community of colours and brush strokes each helping all the others to make a thing of beauty which, at the same time, reflects the beauty of God - the loveliness of the creator and the created. Gothic architecture was also based on the Law of Help: human communities worked together for centuries, generation after generation, to build a cathedral. The builders were all slightly different but united by belief in a God imminent in the world. An eternal spiritual unity underlay their worldly variety but each workman expressed his own being and so was fulfilled and whole. The Middle Ages, in fact, got the balance right between life, art, work and the numinous and therefore medieval masons were in tune with nature in a way that we are not. All great ages are spiritual, as is all great art, and the Middle Ages were both. Out of a wholeness of life, work, and the spiritual came the Cathedrals, the immaterial encased in stone, a fusion of earth and heaven.

The Renaissance put paid to all that by breaking the connection between the spiritual and the everyday through "insolent atheism" and a new kind of rigid, blueprint architecture which denied creativity to the builders who could no longer take joy in what they did. This new style of architecture, Ruskin writes in *The Stones of Venice,* is "Pagan in its origin, proud and unholy in its revival, paralysed in its old age... an architecture invented, as it seems, to make plagiarists of its architects, slaves of its workmen, and sybarites of its inhabitants; an architecture in which intellect is idle, invention impossible, but in which all luxury is gratified and all insolence fortified."

England's Industrial Revolution* made things worse and the Victorians had it all wrong - man was pitted against man in defiance of the universal Law of Cooperation: capitalists degraded their workers through greed and worship of the "Goddess of Getting On". Long days spent doing the same thing over and over again in mills and factories dehumanised men, women and children. "It is a sad account of a man to give of himself that he has spent his life in opening a valve, and never made anything but the eighteenth part of a pin."

Architecture expresses the spirit of the age and England's mill towns showed up the meanness at the heart of the new one. Ruskin was also the first, as far as I know, to see that ugliness is destructive. Ugliness - mental and environmental - left factory and mill hands stunted and un-self-actualised, culturally impoverished, cut off from the eternity which was theirs by right. Industrial ugliness kills something of supreme value in a person.

Ruskin also argued that the modern world is commodified - things are more important that values - and what isn't measurable isn't worthwhile. People should dedicate their work to God, use materials according to their natures, treat beauty as an aspiration to the divine. Things should be made with joy and with a proper concern for a country's history, with no pointless striving for originality but simply to evolve civilisation. All great art is made only by cohesive societies based on a shared common faith, law, language, a common sense of belonging. But, we can add, with enough difference and inner tension to prevent stagnation and allow advancement and evolution*.

Becoming a whole, self-completed person is more important than wages: "The highest reward for a person's toil is not what they get for it, but what they become by it," as he put it.

"There is no wealth but life. Life including all its powers of love, of joy, and of admiration. That country is the richest which nourishes the greatest number of noble and happy human beings; that man is richest who, having perfected the functions of his own life to the utmost, has also the widest helpful influence, both personal, and by means of his possessions, over the lives of others." He summed it all up in a single sentence in the last volume of *Modern Painters*: "Government and co-operation are in all things the Laws of Life; anarchy and competition the Laws of Death."

He outlined some of these ideas in four essays in the *Cornhill* magazine in 1860. He intended more but the public outcry was such that the editor - Thackeray no less - panicked and cancelled them. They were published two years later as *Unto This Last*. This book is usually regarded as the founding document of the Welfare State although of course he didn't present the world with a ready made blueprint - more a scatter of ideas which others then worked on. William Morris said: "He seemed to point out a new road on which others should travel".

Ruskin was an anti-capitalist* in spite of the fact that the rich men who drank his father's sherry freed him to think, travel, and write. He saw capitalism as materialist and the cause of standardisation which stopped people from becoming self-actualised. Capitalism, he thought, couldn't cater for the non-standard man but instead created conformist stereotypes. Adam Smith's division of labour alienated the worker because it broke the need to make something whole and complete. He was also against Smith and Mill because he thought they were materialists and utilitarians and there was more to life than those withered philosophies.

Redistribution is still popular among many people but some of Ruskin's other ideas are just slightly odd - private employers should hire the best workers while the state employs the rest in Government-owned factories, to complement, not compete.

He accepted the cake fallacy - the size of the economy is fixed, not growable, and so whoever takes a bigger slice robs the rest.

Yet he also believed in small-scale, State-free, privately run cooperatives and he was no mere theorist either - he backed up his ideas with his own money: for a couple of years in the 1870s, two of his mother's old servants ran a tea shop he set up in London, selling the leaf rather than the liquid kind. He was himself a slum landlord, having inherited a few tenements in St Marylebone from his father. Octavia Hill, one of the founders of the National Trust, ran them for him for a time, on sound principles: part of the rent money, which was low, was spent on repairs. He hired men, among them one of his own gardeners and a shoe-shine boy, to sweep the street-crossings of the Seven Dials rookery (or outside the British Museum, accounts vary). His Guild of St George bought land in the country to farm cooperatively on Ruskinian principles. The Guild still exists: it has a museum in Sheffield and owns woodland in the Wyre Forest in Worcestershire. He tried, we're told, to bring spinning back to the Isle of Man and printing to Orpington. He taught in Working Men's Colleges and got Oxford undergraduates to mend a road at the foot of the Cumnor Hills in 1874. (The work wasn't very well done, according to Oscar Wilde, who was there. The idea behind it was that everybody should be taught manual trades as well as book learning. Idle upper class girls should make dresses for their working class sisters - they should also get up early and do some housework. Gentlemen should be able to work the lands they owned with their own hands.)

By 1870, now in his fifties, he worried that his ideas were being ignored: his answer was a monthly newsletter - *Fors Clavigera: Letters to the Workmen and Labourers of Great Britain** (1871-84). He wrote them between bouts of the madness which closed down the last ten years of his life. In 1886 they were reissued as books. *Letter 37* (1874) perhaps sums up his position. One day on his way to lecture on Florentine Fine Art in the

University's Gallery in Oxford he stopped to watch a little working class girl whipping a top: she wore a woman's broken shoes three sizes too big. The lecture was one of his best but what did it matter? How can rich and comfortable, well-dressed, well-fed, well-housed people be transported by art in a world which treats impoverished little girls without pity or compassion?

In 1906, six years after Ruskin's death, the new Liberal Government under LLoyd George started to lay out the beginnings of a Welfare State. In 1908, for example, it brought in pensions for the over seventies - from one shilling to five shillings a week at a time when a navvy's wage was sixpence an hour. By 1920, only twenty years after Ruskin's death, Howard Whitehouse, President of the Ruskin Society, claimed that many of his ideas had already been realised: "They include policies relating to land and reform, the methods of dealing with slums, modern methods of taxation, the scientific treatment of such problems as unemployment, sweating, the care of the aged poor, the hours and conditions of labour and the relations between capital and labour, the reform of our educational system, the planning of cities and many others." In *Ruskin the Prophet and Other Centenary Studies* (1920) he lists some of the people Ruskin influenced - from Trade Unionists and writers (Eliot, Chesterton, Yeats, Pound) to William Morris's arts and crafts movement and architects such as Corbusier, Sullivan, Lloyd Wright, Gropius*. And even the Olympic Games which Pierre de Coubertin based on Ruskinian ideas of beauty.

It used to be said that in its early days the British Labour Party was more Methodist than Marxist however it seems it was more Ruskinian than either: Ruskin influenced both Beveridge and Atlee, the men who probably did most to set up the Welfare State after the Second World War.

For all his concern for the workers, Ruskin was no egalitarian: he called himself a Tory-Communist but in reality what he had in mind was a Thomas More-like Utopia. He had two masters: Plato and Thomas Carlyle (1795-1881). Like Carlyle, like Plato, he didn't think people were equal and didn't deserve too much freedom - instead, they had to be ruled by an elite: Carlyle favoured strong men, alpha-males, heroes. Ruskin also believed in the "great man theory" - some people are so innately superior and exalted they have the right to "compel and subdue their inferiors" - but hoped the ruling class of landowners and capitalists of his day could be civilised into becoming trustees of the common good. What he never anticipated, I suspect, that the Welfare State would be so materialist, in both meanings of the word, and that the connection between beauty and the divine would be broken.

CHAPTER X

Ruskin the Platonist

*Platonism is a genuine faith, a living interpretation of life,
by which men have guided their conduct and moulded their
thoughts.*

DEAN INGE

Ruskin distinguished between *theoria* and *aesthetics*. Aesthetics,
as I understand it, is like Gilpin's picturesque prettiness whereas
theoria is the beauty that joins you to the Platonic *Is*.

When he was four, his nurse took him to Friar's Crag above
Derwentwater in Westmorland and there he had what he called
his first mystical experience. Years later he recalled the "intense
joy, mingled with awe, I had in looking through the hollows in
the mossy roots, over the crag, into the dark lake." His "destiny",
however, was fixed by another spiritual experience at the age of
fourteen when, from a terrace above the Rhine, he saw the Alps
in the far distance "like the rose-tinted walls of Eden". Another
(one of many) experience came to him, in his mid-twenties, in
the Chamonix valley in Switzerland. A thunder storm raged
below the high, serene, unmoved, sunlit, peaks which were "the
very heart of heaven - a celestial city with walls of amethyst and
gates of gold - filled with the light and clothed with the Peace

of God". For the first time he really understood beauty. To see it you must "turn the human soul from gazing upon itself". "It was only then I understood that to become nothing might be to become more than Man."

The Chamonix valley was the Eden from which he was never expelled while Geneva was his Yeatsian Byzantium where eternity came down to earth, the still point of his turning world - lake, Rhone, Erve, Mont Blanc, sycamore shaded walks and M. Bautte's jeweller's workshop. The Rhone - a liquid glacier rather than a river - reflected the goldsmith's wares as its "currents twisted the light into golden braids, and inlaid the threads with turquoise enamel".

Landscape, more particularly high mountains, opened up the vision of God or eternity for him. "The one who loves nature most," he wrote, "will always be found to have more faith in God than the other." And: "nature-worship ... becomes the channel to sacred truth, which by no other means can be conveyed." Beautiful things were like windows through which he could see what he called God, though he realised it went deeper than organised religion: the vision is primary while what you make of it is cultural and secondary.

Art could and should act in the same way. Ruskin's father, for example, collected Turner's work long before the painter was famous. As a boy Ruskin saw through them to God beyond. In his early twenties, in fact, he began his career by defending Turner in *Modern Painters* (1843-1860). Unlike earlier landscape artists, such as Poussin or Lorrain, Turner's art is a gateway to the divinity which is abroad in the world because he saw nature as it really is and painted what he saw - the "truth of water", "truth of tone", "truth of colour". If beauty comes in through the eye, then people have to be taught to look and to see. How? Through awareness of detail. Examples of what he meant can be taken almost at random from *Modern Painters* - Turner's water-fall in Upper Teesdale, for instance. Foam is easy to fake, Ruskin claimed; scuffing the paper lightly is one way, crumbling white paint on it another. A leap of water is not hard to do, either. But what Turner paints is the "tumble" of water - its unhindered drop from rock lip to pool. He catches not just the laciness but also the permanent patterns made by freely falling water.

Natural colour is important, too. To show its misuse Ruskin chose a painting in the National Gallery in London - Salvator Rosa's *Mercury and the dishonest woodman.* The distant mountains are blue but detailed (you can see the crags and the cracks in the rock) although in nature any mountain far enough away to look blue will also be featureless. Turner never did anything so crass. Like nature herself his distant mountains are sapphire blue and smooth.

An artist should be a metaphysician attaching time to eternity. By absorbing art via a quietened mind we open ourselves to the unseen. Good art is spiritual and connects us to eternity, or God. Sadness and repose are also at the centre of all great art which, in turn, is made only by cohesive societies sharing a common faith, law, language, a common sense of belonging. Without a sense of the invisible you can't get to the essence of what is beautiful and turn it into great poetry, painting or music. Art is also a touchstone by which we judge the health of a society. What is deep inside people shows up in their art. If they are brutal, degraded, ugly, shallow or empty, so will their art be.

But Ruskin was also appalled by his own time. Modern art was a kind of anxiety, he said. He called his own century an Age of Umber and thought the darkness of the times was caused by a lack of faith, or the loss of a wholeness of outlook. Where the Greeks saw gods in the woods, the Victorians saw poachers; where the Middle Ages saw angels in the clouds, the Victorians predicted rain. The result was plainly seeable in the age's debased art and architecture.

Yet, paradoxically, he also recognised the greatness of Wordsworth, Tennyson, Carlyle, Browning - and even Pugin:

after all, between them they launched the Gothic Revival. He also stood up for one of the century's great art movements. In 1848 seven very young men set up the Pre-Raphaelite Brotherhood. Chief among them were William Holman Hunt (1827-1910), John Everett Millais (1829-1896) and Dante Gabriel Rossetti (18281882). They were in rebellion against the ruling elite and, wanting to start again from a better base, went back to the days before Raphael to painters like Giotto (1267-1337) and the naturalistic simplicity of his post-Byzantine but pre-Renaissance times. They were all very young: in 1848 Ruskin was only twenty-nine, while Rossetti (the youngest) was twenty and still legally a minor, I believe. (Their predecessors, *The Ancients*, just over twenty years earlier also harked back to the past to make a new start.)

Ruskin certainly championed the PRB: in a letter to *The Times* in 1851 he wrote: "with all their faults, their pictures are since Turner's death the best, the incomparably best, on the walls of the Royal Academy." But did his ideas influence their work? Holman Hunt certainly said so, early in the 20th century, when he recalled that in the late 1840s he'd skimmed through a borrowed copy of *Modern Painters I*, in his bedroom, and been instantly struck by the passage which tells painters to "go to Nature in all singleness of heart, and walk with her laboriously and trustingly, having no other thoughts but how best to penetrate her meaning, and remember her instructions; rejecting nothing, selecting nothing, and scorning nothing; believing all things to be right and good, and rejoicing always in the truth". Holman Hunt goes on to claim he then convinced the rest of the Brotherhood.

Some years after this Ruskin again pointed Holman Hunt (there were three with the same surname) in a new direction - typological painting. Ruskin discovered it, I think, when he studied Tintoretto's *Annunciation* (1583-87) in Venice. Typology is prophetic symbolism - symbols pointing to what is to be, foretelling a future which is already known. In Tintoretto's painting the Virgin sits in a ruined house with angels and carpenter's tools: the old religion has decayed and fallen apart, a new one is about to be born and built.

When it came to painting landscapes in the open air, nature in all its detail didn't do too well in England's fickle weather, particularly before the invention of the portable paint which helped the Impressionists. The PRB turned more to narrative painting, medieval and moody, religious scenes, scenes from poetry, Camelot and beautiful women.

The PRB didn't last long but their influence evolved until it all ebbed away into art for art's sake (though art, of course, is for eternity's sake or to help grow the mind) at the century's end. By the early 20th century, they - and most things Victorian - were scorned and derided. In a reversal of that, Ruskin disliked later painters like Whistler. Of Whistler's *Nocturne in Black and Gold: The Falling Rocket* he wrote: "I have seen, and heard, much of Cockney impudence before now but never expected to hear a coxcomb ask two hundred guineas for flinging a pot of paint in the public's face." Whistler sued for libel, won a farthing in damages and was ruined.

I'm not sure if Ruskin ever mentioned the Impressionists (he wrote thirty-nine books, some very long and often long-winded) although he did influence them, at least according to Monet who said "ninety percent of the theory of Impressionist painting is in *Elements of Drawing*" (1857) about the need to study nature closely and faithfully.

Ruskin, I suspect, was a Christian and a Platonist rather than a Christian-Platonist. In fact, he was a Christian twice over. Like many Victorians, he lost his faith. According to one account, the cause was geology, not Darwin - Lyell's *Principles of Geology* was published in 1833 when Ruskin was twenty-four. "Those dreadful hammers!" he complained. "If only the geologists would let me alone!" The earth is very old, Lyell had discovered: in the Bible it's very very young. (Oddly enough, Ruskin was a member of the Geological Society of London, founded 1807, and many of his sketches are of rocks.) The final split came suddenly in a Waldensian chapel in Turin in 1858. The preacher, "a little squeaking idiot", told his congregation (seventeen old women, "three louts", and Ruskin) they were only people in the city who were saved. Moments before Ruskin had been looking at Veronese's lusty Queen of Sheba. The contrast between the painter's largeness of mind and the bitter smallness of the preacher was too much.

A few years later, looking for peace, he regained a kind of self-made non-Evangelical Christianity - pushed, it seems, by a seance just before Christmas, 1875, when the ghost of Rose la Touche was said to have appeared, though not to him. The following March he wrote: "I have no new faith, but am able to get some good out of my old one, not as being true, but as containing the quantity of truth that is wholesome for me". What he now believed was simple and very un-abstract: God is, God made, God came, God suffered, God died, God rose and will come again to judge - except there is a Heaven but no Hell. (Hell came again all its Puritan fury when he finally went mad and fought the Devil and all his evils. Ten years earlier he said the Devil exists but it is us, or in us.)

Why was Platonism not enough? Perhaps because his experiences were big and few, not minor and many, the Alps, not shadows on a whitewashed wall. He missed, in other words, daily undertones of eternity.

He wasn't a self-examined man and never asked why he was the way he was. In England introspection, in fact, was thought unhealthy well into the 20th century.

Or perhaps Inge was right: "I have often been surprised that Ruskin was not a more whole-hearted admirer of Wordsworth, considering how they shared their love of the beautiful Lake country, but I imagine that Ruskin was not a philosophic mystic in the sense which Plato was and Wordsworth was. He touches Plato on another side, one on which Wordsworth had very little interest, the side of practical, political and social reform, based no doubt on a belief in the good and the beautiful."

In other words Ruskin was a practical man who turned his insights into utilitarian use (though he despised Utilitarianism). "Does this make us bigger and better?" is the only question people need ask, and it applies to everything, politics and art in particular. The idea is a distant echo of Aristotle who thought life is about growth - physical, moral, intellectual, spiritual. The end of human life is entelechy - a state of being when all that is good and potential inside you has been actualised. The result is fulfilment or eudemony, a life lived well.

The immaterial is more important than the material, he also said, putting the world in its proper place. In 1888 - "beneath the cloudless peace of the snows of Chamonix" - he wrote the Epilogue to *Modern Painters* and in it reaffirmed his lifelong intuition that the abstract beauty of that self same world is both sacred and eternal.

PART THREE

—

Decline and Fall

CHAPTER I

Wordsworth Platonised

Wordsworth's poetry is of a spiritual experience so intense, so pure, and so profound that it holds the essence of all religion. The text of the early Prelude gives us that elemental experience freed from the gloss of later interpretation. And it shows us, further, how its roots lay, where Wordsworth did not shrink from finding them, in the sensuous life which is our common heritage.

He was a poet with a powerful mind, not a trained philosopher, and his thought does not lend itself to analytical exposition. It was itself the expression of a richly endowed nature: it grows with his growth, and is full of complexities and contradictions.

The mysterious, endless, quickening power of suffering is a cardinal theme of Wordsworth's poetry.

Places haunted his imagination as much as people.

Coleridge was the friend of his genius as well as of his heart. It was Coleridge who made him believe in the value of what he had to say as a poet, and who helped him to understand it in terms of thought. Wordsworth never forgot it.

HELEN DARBISHIRE

Wordsworth was born in 1770 in Cockermouth, a small Cumberland market town where the River Cocker meets the Derwent. His father, a lawyer, was factor to the Sir James Lowther who was later raised to the peerage as the Earl of Lonsdale. (The 5th Earl originated the Lonsdale Belt for boxing in 1909.) Lonsdales still own the castle above the gorge at a bend in the River Lowther, a tributary of the Eden. The first earl cheated Wordsworth senior out of four thousand pounds of wages. The second handed over the stolen money but only after being sued by the Wordsworth family, both fathers being dead by then.

Wordsworth's mother died when he was eight. His father (who died only five years later) was unable to cope and packed William and his brother Richard off to the Grammar School in Hawkshead, a small stone or slate built village, quaint and picturesque in a hard kind of way, in the Vale of Esthwaite. William was only eight or nine when he went there and he was allowed to be pretty wild and free: skating, climbing, flying kites, scrambling about in hazel trees gathering nuts, snaring, (poaching), swimming, boating, horseback riding (galloping along the sands of the Leven at midnight, and by moonlight.) Those are the Platonist days chronicled in *The Prelude* and alluded to as lost in the *Immortality Ode*.

From the boarding school in Hawkshead Wordsworth went to Penrith where he was less free and therefore less happy - he admitted to an "over-love of freedom." (It was here he met Mary Hutchinson, his future wife.) When he was seventeen he went to Cambridge - to Newton's old college, St John's - where he was like a bird "ill-tutored for captivity." "I was detached internally from academic cares." He was, he also said, "not for that hour, not for that place." Examinations at that time revolved around the Mathematical Tripos and the whole university was like a clearing house for would-be clerics fawning for preferment. Aping your betters - emulation - was encouraged but, said Wordsworth, "I can sincerely affirm, that I am not indebted to emulation for my attainments, whatever they may be. I have from my youth cultivated the habit of valuing knowledge for its own sake."

Undergraduates wasted their mornings dressing as dandies and then carousing and rioting into the small hours. Thomas Gray, the poet, wrote that they turn "women upon their heads in the streets at noon, break open shops and game in the coffee houses on Sundays" while *The Tuns Tavern* was "the scene of nightly orgies in which professors and fellows set an example of roistering to the youth of the university". Twelve years before Wordsworth went up, his fellow poet, William Cowper wrote that the place was full of "gamesters, jockeys, brothellers impure, spendthrifts and booted sportsmen". Wordsworth caroused as well but perhaps more prudishly (in fact was almost a teetotaller).

What he didn't do, after the first year, was study: he went this own way, reading what he wanted. When he was eighteen "vows were made for him" - that is, he knew poetry was his calling - yet it was nearly another ten years before he found his twin themes - extrovertive nature mysticism and the revolutionising of poetry and, through it, social reform. In his third year he and his Welsh friend, Robert Jones, took three months off to trek three thousand miles through France and Switzerland, their bundles on their heads, buying a boat to float back down the Rhine on their way home (they took twenty pounds with them). He graduated with a poor degree and drifted for four years. In London he heard Burke speak in the House of Commons, saw Mrs Siddons on stage, and watched the city crowds. Poetry, he was to say later, is "emotion recollected in tranquillity". In 1806 he recollected, in tranquillity, the stillness of London in the still hours of a silent morning:

Ne'er saw I, never felt, a calm so deep!
The river glideth at his own sweet will:
Dear God! the very houses seem asleep;
And all that mighty heart is lying still!

He crossed to Revolutionary France late in 1791 and stayed through most of 1792, the year which saw the end of the monarchy, the rise of the Republic, and the September Massacres. Either in Orleans or Blois, he met Annette Vallon: they had a daughter, Caroline. (He saw daughter and mother only once again, during the Peace of Amiens: Annette never married and was always known as the Widow Williams, Wordsworth being unpronounceable in French.) His money ran out as he was about to join the Girondins so he caught the ferry to Dover.

Before then, however, he met Michel Armand Beaupuy (1755-1796), an aristocratic republican from Périgord, and a captain in a Royalist infantry regiment. At Blois in the Loire valley, he turned Wordsworth into a revolutionary, a believer in fraternity, liberty and (illogically) equality. In *The Prelude* the episode is shortened into a brief story: Beaupuy points to a "hunger-bitten" girl knitting as she creeps along a lane, a grazing heifer tied by a cord to her arm: that kind of poverty, he said, is what we're fighting *against*. "I became a patriot," Wordsworth said, "and my heart was all Given to the people and my love was theirs".

Inevitably Wordsworth was disillusioned when the revolution turned into terror and wars of conquest. Back in England he briefly flirted with Godwinism - met the man himself - but soon recoiled from its abuse of reason. William Godwin (1756-1836) - "the founder of philosophical anarchism" - was an early example of extreme collectivism: reason will make us immortal once we get rid of property, marriage, money, laws, Government and the family (though he was a bit put out when his daughter ran off with the already married Shelley). But Wordsworth found feelings to be deeper and truer than reason. In his un-actable play, *The Borderers*, the villain Oswald "banishes feeling" and "incites the hero, Marmaduke, to fiendish crime in the name of Reason".

Some time before this, he'd nursed or briefly been a companion to a young man, Raisley Calvert, who was dying of tuberculosis, near Keswick. Raisley, believing Wordsworth had the makings of a great poet, left him nine hundred pounds in his will. Two other friends, the Pinney brothers, gave him the rent-free use of Racedown Lodge, a recently built small country mansion isolated on a hill under an Iron Age fort in Dorset not far from Lyme Bay. He went there with his sister, Dorothy. They ate well when the Pinney boys came down, otherwise they lived off "essence of carrots, cabbages and turnips" which they grew themselves.

Basil Montagu paid them twenty shillings a week to look after his son, also called Basil, whose mother had died giving birth to him. (Basil Senior, a friend from Cambridge, was an illegitimate son of the Earl of Sandwich. His mother had been an opera singer until an enraged Vicar from Norwich, a one time lover, shot her dead outside Covent Garden Opera House.) The boy was an expert liar, apparently, and appears as such in *Lyrical Ballads*. Mary Hutchinson, among others, visited and stayed.

Then Samuel Taylor Coleridge (1772-1834) walked all the way from Somerset to meet and persuade them to move to the Quantock Hills where he lived at the time. In the summer of 1797 the Wordsworths rented a small mansion, Alfoxden House, at the north-western end of the range, three or four miles over the hill from Coleridge's Nether Stowey. The Quantock is probably best called a plateau, a thousand feet high, twelve miles long, three or four wide. All the same, Dorothy said the area had everything. It still has: "wild simplicity", steep combes (wet, deep, green,) delicate with moss, dense with woods of slender trees, and flowing with stony brooks like the becks back home in Cumberland. Exmoor can usually be seen, blue in the distance. The Bristol Channel is only a few miles from the house, close enough to hear the sea breaking in storms.

Wordsworth and his sister were separated in childhood and were now together for the first time. (After their mother's death, Dorothy was brought up by a second cousin in Halifax while

William ran wild in Westmorland.) John Campbell Shairp -
who in 1874 edited her *Tour* of Scotland - wrote: "She discerned
his real need and divined the remedy. By her cheerful society,
fine tact, and vivid love of nature she turned him, depressed
and bewildered, alike from abstract speculations and the contemporary politics in which he had got himself immersed, and
directed his thoughts towards the truth of poetry, and the face of
nature, and the healing that for him lay in these." Wordsworth
himself wrote:

> She gave me eyes, she gave me ears;
> And humble cares, and delicate fears;
> A heart, the fountain of sweet tears;
> And love, and thought, and joy.

Time and again in her *Journal*, Dorothy illustrates their
shared lifelong interest in people and nature (as well as a sensitivity to the beauty of landscape). 23 Feb 1798, still in Somerset:
"Wm. and I walked after dinner to Woodlands: the moon and
two planets: sharp and frosty. Met a razor-grinder with a soldier's jacket on, a knapsack upon his back, and a boy to drag the
wheel. The sea very black, and making a loud noise as we came
through the wood, loud as if disturbed, and the wind silent."

If were her brother's Platonist half, then Coleridge was his
Hellenist: she drew Wordsworth back to nature, to beauty or
Arnoldian sweetness, while Coleridge showed him the light of
the intellect which sees life steadily and sees it whole. They were
"three persons with one soul". The two young men (aged twenty-five and twenty-seven) were very different temperamentally
but together they thrashed out a kind of working philosophy for Wordsworth. "Coleridge's penetrating mind lit up for
Wordsworth the true meaning of his own mental experiences,"
as Helen Darbishire puts in the preface to her collection of
pieces from *The Prelude* (1927). In *The Poet Wordsworth* she adds:

Coleridge was "a Library-Cormorant …tormented by philosophical problems." Wordsworth "explored where Coleridge wanted to get things right".

Between them sister and friend brought out what was inherent in Wordsworth, clarified and made it articulate, something he seemed incapable of doing for himself. They made explicit the Way of Beauty and the Intellect. Ultimate meaning is deeper than reason or revolution, down where eternity breaks through matter. Coleridge introduced him to *esemplastic power* - the mind's gift for sensing eternity.

Those long talks - and equally long walks - reached a conclusion early in 1798 and the first, short, edition of *Lyrical Ballads* was written that Spring and summer ready for printing in the Autumn. It introduced Romanticism to England, with a new kind of poetry - personal and emotional, in freer language - not dry, distant, classical and orderly like the verse of the passing Age of Reason. Wordsworth also wrote the famous Preface explaining that the new diction of their poetry was based on ballads and "the real language of men". On top of that, all modern and modernist poetry in English stems from those few days and months in Somerset.

The two young men also originated not only a new kind of blank verse but a new iconography: no longer the gods but the poor, downtrodden, outcast: beggars, dispossessed peasants, leech-gatherers, discharged soldiers, the old, the odd, the idiot. Most of the of the poems are stories about the rural poor when poverty meant real daily hunger if not downright starvation and many people were under five feet tall and life expectancy was less than forty. We can take two of his poems almost at random to show Wordsworth's outlook: *Goody Blake and Harry Gill* (pity) and *Peter Bell* (goodness at the heart of nature). Harry Gill is a young and comfortable drover: Goody Blake is a poor lonely old woman who lives in a hovel on the Quantock Hills barely eking out a living by spinning wool. In the bitter cold of winter she creeps down to gather twigs from Harry's hedge to feed her pitiful little fire. Harry catches her and Goody asks God to make him never feel warm again, even at the height of summer:

> The cold, cold moon above her head,
> Thus on her knees did Goody pray;
> Young Harry heard what she had said:
> And icy cold he turned away.

Peter Bell, as big a scoundrel as ever lived, hawks pots for a living all over the island. One night he stumbles on a donkey by the River Swale. He tries to lead it away and steal it. The donkey won't budge. He beats it. The donkey falls down. Then Peter Bell sees a corpse in the river, the donkey's drowned master. Bell faints and when he recovers he pulls the dead man out of the water and the donkey licks his hand in gratitude. The donkey then carries Bell to the dead man's home. On the way things happen to change him. For example, he remembers a Scottish girl, one of his many wives, who died of a broken heart, having named the baby in her womb Benoni, the Child of Sorrow. Bell has no experience of eternity and is redeemed solely by the upwelling of the decency and innate love which lies deep in all of us because we are all part of the unity of nature:

> A primrose by a river's brim
> A yellow primrose was to him,
> And it was nothing more.
>
> The soft blue sky did never melt
> Into his heart; he never felt
> The witchery of the soft blue sky!

In April 1798 the Government, shocked by what the French were up to, suspended Habeas Corpus and then banned the Corresponding Societies. The Home Office spied on radicals such as Coleridge and Wordsworth (or so the story goes). Their private spook, a bit of a yokel, told London that their Controller was called Spy Nozy - Spinoza being Coleridge's latest philosophical fad. Lady St Albyn, the Tory who owned Alfoxden House, refused to renew the lease when it ended in June, 1798, and the Wordsworths were expelled.

All three spent the winter of 1798/9, the coldest of the century, in Germany. They split up and the Wordsworths went to a small town which Wordsworth described in a letter to Josiah Wedgwood: "Goslar is a venerable ... decayed city. It is situated at the foot of some small mountains, on the edge of the Harts forest. It was once the residence of Emperors, and is now the residence of Grocers and Linen-drapers who are, I say it with a feeling of sorrow, a wretched race; the flesh, blood, and bone of their minds being nothing by knavery and low falshood."

The Wordsworths were isolated, unable to speak German or even to learn it. But Coleridge had persuaded William to write a long poem about philosophy to be called *The Recluse, or Views of Nature, Man and Society*. He outlined the theme in a letter: it would refute "the sandy Sophisms of Locke and the Mechanic Dogmatists, and demonstrating that the senses are living growths and developments of the Mind and Spirit." It would also falsify Erasmus Darwin's theory of evolution (his grandson, Charles, later gave us Natural Selection to explain how it works). Man didn't evolve from "Ouran Outangs" but he did fall and *The Recluse*, if I understand Coleridge correctly, should follow the rise of self-awareness to the present day.

Before then, as a prelude, Wordsworth had to set out his credentials, his authority, for writing such a poem - an autobiography, something new in verse, chronicling the "growth of a poet's mind". He began writing it in Somerset, carried on in

Germany and finished it in in 1805 though he never published or even titled it. For forty-five years it was known in the family as "the poem for Coleridge". His widow published the over-worked-over poem as *The Prelude* after her husband's death in 1850. *The Excursion*, the only part of the *Recluse* to be written, came out in 1814.

There are only twenty-four poems in the 1798 edition of *Lyrical Ballads*, which opens with Coleridge's *Rime of the Ancient Mariner* and ends with *Tintern Abbey:* book-ended, in fact, by the supernatural and the numinous. *Lyrical Ballads* went through another three editions, gaining pieces as it went, and shedding Coleridge on the way. The 1801 edition had the famous Preface about poetry being "the spontaneous overflow of powerful feelings … recollected in tranquillity". The last edition came out in 1805.

Poems, 1807 are different again. Helen Darbishire wrote: "In the *Lyrical Ballads* Wordsworth had turned his back on his personal life and had made something like a strenuous voyage of discovery, a sort of arctic expedition, into a region where life was reduced to his elements, the outward trappings to their simplest: his aim to penetrate the heart of man and the inner life of nature. In the *Poems* of 1807 he is back in the world of his own personal life and thought."

The Platonist/mystical poems are *Tintern Abbey* (in *Lyrical Ballads*), *Ode: Intimations of Immortality* (in *Poems, 1807*) and in Books I, II and XIII of the 1805 edition of *The Prelude*. But constant revision, re-writing and Christianising over the years damaged *The Prelude's* Platonist roots and so reduced its value. Helen Darbishire puts it: "The middle-aged Wordsworth who revised *The Prelude* was betrayed by the ineradicable weakness of civilised man: he had to explain, to rationalise, to moralise. Moreover, since he was not only a civilised but a deeply religious man, and a devout adherent of the Anglican Church, he had to translate his thoughts into the terms of an orthodox Christian creed." For example, to take perhaps the most extreme example, of the fifteen words in these two 1805 lines only five survived in 1850 and one of those is *the*:

> *The feeling of* life endless (the *great* thought
> *By which we live) infinity* and God.

> *Faith in* life endless (the *sustaining* thought
> *Of human being) eternity* and God.

By a strange coincidence 1850, the exact mid-century, was a cross-over point - Wordsworth died and Tennyson took over the Laureateship from him: Wordsworth's *Prelude* appeared in print as did Tennyson's *In Memoriam* - the one a redacted Georgian poem, the other purely Victorian. Tennyson - a lifelong mystic - asks is there an afterlife and a God who cares? Answer: choose to believe and have faith. In the 1805 *Prelude* Wordsworth gives a different answer: you're one and the same as eternity itself. Unfortunately this edition was unknown until 1926 when its kind of Platonism was in any case largely forgotten. What might have been happened if it and *In Memoriam* had appeared at the same time? The following year, 1851, Matthew Arnold composed *Dover Beach* about the ebbing away of Christianity from Victorian England.

CHAPTER II

The De-Platonising
of William Wordsworth

Inevitably those first incomparable experiences of his childhood, when sense and soul were one, grew less and less frequent. The sense-experience began to separate itself from the spiritual.

HELEN DARBISHIRE

Platonism is based on an experience which can occur long before the experiencer has a name for it. For some, those experiences stop in adulthood. Without a name the whole thing can then end, whereas a label of some kind could turn it into a living philosophy. J A Stewart called Wordsworth a *Personal* Platonist because he never specifically described himself as such. When the experiences of his childhood and early adulthood ended, he had no name for them and so they were lost, along - it can be argued - with his talent or genius. For consolation he took up a slightly heretical Anglican form of Christianity. If he'd had a named philosophy how different might the last fifty years of his life have been? Deeper? Would he have still been a major poet?

There was, perhaps, another factor - his contact with what he called divinity was direct, by-passing the beauty which is always ready to remind and reconnect. Without the recurring vision via beauty there was little to keep it active and alive.

Whatever the cause we can trace the weakening and loss of his intuition through the poetry and - more speculatively - his domestic life. As early as 1804, at the height of his talent and still only thirty-four, he wrote *Intimations of Immortality*:

> There was a time when meadow, grove, and stream,
> The earth, and every common sight,
> To me did seem
> Apparelled in celestial light,
> The glory and the freshness of a dream.
>
> But now...
> Whither is fled the visionary gleam?
> Where is it now, the glory and the dream?
>
> At length the Man perceives it die away,
> And fade into the light of common day.
>
> And yet something of the power of the glory is still there:
>
> Those shadowy recollections,
> Which, be they what they may
> Are yet the fountain-light of all our day,
> Are yet a master-light of all our seeing.
>
> But not for very long.

Early in the 19th century, the 2nd Earl of Lonsdale paid the Wordsworths the money his father owned them, which meant William could marry. By 1804, when he wrote *Intimations of Immortality*, he had two children: John (1803) and Dora (1804). Three more followed - Thomas (1806), Catherine (1808) and William (1810). Did the domesticity of family life help to end his vision?

That end was already in sight when his sister, Dorothy, began her Grasmere *Journal* on 14th May 1800 (a Wednesday) with Wordsworth and their sailor brother, John, setting off with pork in their pockets at half past two in the afternoon to go to Gallow Hill near Scarborough to visit Mary Hutchinson, who was to become Wordsworth's wife two years later. (The *Journal* ends on Sunday 16th January 1803 with Dorothy going on an "intensely cold day", wearing Molly's cloak and her own spencer, to buy gingerbread for her brother from Michael Newton, a blind man sitting in his Sabbath clothes with his wife and sister. The gingerbread cost sixpence.)

The old way of living was already crossing over with the new. Coleridge was still there, near them in the Lake District. (On Thursday 10th June 1802, Dorothy records that a cow attacked him as he came over from Grisedale with a bag of books and a branch of mountain ash. It was a day of "furious wind", and Wordsworth was ill.)

Above all, her brother's marriage sidelined Dorothy - the other person who'd helped Wordsworth flourish as poet. (Curiously, soon after the wedding, Wordsworth, Coleridge and Dorothy set off together on a tour of Scotland in a jaunting car*.) She'd lived her life to the fullest in those seven years when she had her brother all to herself in Somerset, Germany and Grasmere. Then, after his children came along, she more or less settled down to the life of a maiden aunt, a spinster good for nursing the sick or helping with the very young or very old. She was housekeeping for John, Wordsworth's oldest boy (a curate in Leicestershire), when she was taken seriously ill with gall bladder problems, a sickness from which she never really recovered. As we'll see, she died insane.

She was a better prose writer than her brother - the Daffodil poem was cribbed from her *Journal* - and she summed up their pre-marriage life in Grasmere in her entry for Saturday, 27th March 1802: "A divine morning. At breakfast Wm, wrote part of an ode. Mr Olliff sent the dung and Wm. went to work in the garden. We sate all day in the orchard." The poem, so casually mentioned, is the *Immortality Ode*, one of the greatest in the language, and there we have it - manure and the numinous, earth and the unearthly, on a single fine day just after the coming of Spring.

If Wordsworth had been a Platonist in childhood his sister Dorothy was a Christian as defined here: an exemplar of love, self-sacrifice, suffering and forgiveness. She was designed for young adulthood - old age wouldn't have suited her even if she hadn't lost her mind: middle age didn't. She was also a child of place - the Vale of Grasmere, in particular. She needed not only hills but woods and wooded fells, rock outcrops, flowers, lakes (with bays and islands), becks, waterfalls, streams and rivers - a homely familiar landscape which changing weather made end-lessly new. She was generous with what little she had, devoted her life to her brother and his work, had a genius for friendship, disliked grand houses and despised riches, insolence and vulgar-ity: "Mercy me," was her exclamation on seeing the three-storey domed rotunda with a portico on Belle Isle in Windermere. (Wordsworth called it a pepper pot. Gilpin didn't like it, either.)

But of necessity, given the times in which she lived, Dorothy was a "home body". Wednesday 11th October 1801: "Baked bread and giblet pie - put books in order - mended stockings. Put aside dearest C's (Coleridge's) letters, and now at about 7 o'clock we are all sitting by a nice fire - W (Wordsworth) with his book and a candle and Mary writing to Sara." She made bread, cakes, tarts, shoes and mended stockings. Mended old clothes and bound carpets. Ironed, starched. (In time stitched frocks for Coleridge's small son.) Planted, weeded, fished, stuffed fish, rowed, drank tea with neighbours, gave money to beggars and the poor. Sailed and walked: walked everywhere almost daily. (For many years - all those early ones - she had a servant or daily help (she didn't live in) called Molly who was more like a friend. Later she had two.)

Hers was also a world of infinite beauty and pain: she suffered almost daily - certainly weekly - from headaches or toothache. Laudanum, castor oil and vinegar were her remedies. Thursday 4th November 1802: "I scalded my foot with coffee after having been in bed in the afternoon - I was near fainting, and then bad in my bowels. Mary waited upon me till 2 o'clock, then we went to bed and with application of vinegar I was lulled to sleep about 4." Saturday 23rd October 1802: Mary was baking while Dorothy walked with Wordsworth to Langdale Rydale. "We had a heavenly walk, but I came home with toothache and have since that day been confined upstairs, till now namely Saturday 30th October 1802." In other words, a full week in bed with toothache. When she got up all was perfect again: "It is a breathless grey day that leaves the golden woods of autumn quiet in their tranquillity, stately and beautiful in their decaying, the lake is a perfect mirror."

What did she fear? Once she was with Coleridge and Wordsworth in an overcrowded, leaking boat, gunwale deep, on Loch Lomond and that scared her. But otherwise it was cows. "Every horned cow puts me in terror." Once a grazing cow blocked her way for half an hour. "The Cow looked at me and I looked at the Cow and whenever I stirred the Cow gave over eating."

By 1805 Wordsworth's nameless vision had faded but not quite vanished when, in February, their brother John, captain of a merchantman, the *Earl of Abergavenny*, drowned in the wreck of his ship on The Shambles off Portland Bill, a place of strong rip tides. His brother's death seems to have made the concept of Christian suffering more real - and all this while he was completing *The Prelude*, the first two books of which are the greatest hymn to non-Christian mysticism in the language.

We can trace the retreat and loss of Platonism in another poem, *Elegiac Stanzas Suggested by a Picture of Peele Castle in a Storm, Painted by Sir George Beaumont*, written in 1807. Sir George Beaumont, 7th Baronet (1753-1827) was a landowner, amateur artist and - more importantly - a founder of the National Gallery in London. He was also friend of Wordsworth (who once spent a winter on Beaumont's estate near Coleorton in Leicestershire). As an artist Beaumont was a disciple of St Joshua Reynolds (art should ape the Renaissance: landscapes should be idealised, not natural) and was anti-Turner (he died when Ruskin was still a boy). In 1805 he painted *Peele Castle in a Storm*. The castle - a box-like ruin - stands on Piel Island near Barrow-in-Furness in Cumbria. The painting shows a dark tunnel of sea, land and sky ending in a blaze of fierce yellow light, the castle with its brown walls peeling apart on the left and a ship, her masts all but gone, her stern to the viewer as her bows seem to slide into the sea. Wordsworth saw the picture in Beaumont's London house.

The *Elegaic Stanzas* is a poem of two halves: recollections of the way Wordsworth once saw the world, and how he sees things now. He begins by telling us he that once he lived for a month in sight of Piel Castle - four weeks either of rare brilliant weather or a world still lit by his inward light. Had he been a painter he'd have mixed eternity in the paint …

> To express what then I saw; and add the gleam,
> The light that never was, on sea or land,

The gleam had been real but not now, particularly not after his brother drowned in a storm similar to the one in Beaumont's painting. Like Ruskin, Wordsworth was a mystic and a social reformer: each rejected the purer, more abstract aspects of Platonism when the times were bad. Christianity can deal with the world's pain better and Wordsworth goes on to tell us:

> I have submitted to a new control:
> A power is gone, which nothing can restore;
> A deep distress hath humanised my Soul.

More than that he now also rejects the barely remembered old vision for another reason - it revolved around a "heart that lives alone", cut off from its own kind and as such to be pitied for its blindness. Instead he now welcomes …

> … fortitude, and patient cheer,
> And frequent sights of what is to be borne!
> Such sights, or worse, as are before me here.
> Not without hope we suffer and we mourn.

Five years later, the old vision is no longer even mentioned. Grief at the death of two of his children - Thomas and Catherine - in 1812 increased his need for comfort and in *The Excursion* (1817) he reaffirms his faith in God's protective goodness:

> One adequate support
> For the calamities of mortal life
> Exists - one only; an assured belief
> That the procession of our fate, howe'er
> Sad or disturbed, is ordered by a Being
> Of infinite benevolence and power;
> Whose everlasting purposes embrace
> All accidents, converting them to good.

Three years after that, now fifty, he refers to Plato for the one and only time, as far as I can see. In doing so he shows he knows what Platonism is all about but distantly, not personally, a thing of almost academic interest. In the 1820s, he wrote a hundred and thirty-two *Ecclesiastical Sonnets* chronicling the history of the Church in England from its beginning. Plato is mentioned in *Latitudinarianism*. Who speaks for Christianity? The Church or …

... a Platonic Piety confined
To the sole temple of the inward mind?

That Piety is Milton's, a man both physically blind and in
danger of his life from the newly re-installed Royalists ...

Yet not alone, nor helpless to repel
Sad thoughts; for from above the starry sphere
Come secrets, whispered nightly to his ear;
And the pure spirit of celestial light
Shines through his soul, "that he may see and tell
Of things invisible to mortal sight".

That last line and a half is a quotation from Milton. The
vision is now totally some one else's.

Once his instinct for infinity had ended, so did - perhaps as a
consequence - the greatness of his poetry, though with occasional
break-throughs. He regained something of the old brilliance in
the last of *The Duddon Sonnets* (1820). The Sonnets trace the
River Duddon in southern Cumbria from its source to the sea -
the stream is like a snake: sheep graze and doze by a stone circle
sacred to the Druids by a Roman fort: a boy and girl cross the
river on stepping stones: the poet imagines he's laid in Ulpha
churchyard "soothed by the unseen River's gentle roar". The last
sonnet sheds undertones as it flows into a doubtful Christianity:

For, backward, Duddon! as I cast my eyes,
I see what was, and is, and will abide;
Still glides the Stream, and shall for ever glide;
The Form remains, the Function never dies;
While we, the brave, the mighty, and the wise,
We Men, who in our morn of youth defied
The elements, must vanish; - be it so!

Enough, if something from our hands have power
To live, and act, and serve the future hour;
And if, as toward the silent tomb we go,
Through love, through hope, and faith's transcendent dower,
We feel that we are greater than we know.

How consistently a conventional Christian he was is hard to say - judging by *The Duddon Sonnets* and at least one other poem, he may not have believed in an afterlife. By the age of sixty-five his friends were dying: Sir Walter Scott (1832), George Crabbe (1832), Coleridge (1834), Charles Lamb (1834), Felicia Hemans (1835). He ends *Extempore Effusion upon the Death of James Hogg* (1835):

Like clouds that rake the mountain-summits,
Or waves that own no curbing hand,
How fast has brother followed brother,
From sunshine to the sunless land!

You can only do one thing well, he said, and for him that was poetry. He wrote a lot - seventy thousand lines, far too much to be read comfortably - and from his late thirties was a technically skilled worker in verse without the boost the joy of eternity once gave him. Sometimes he even reverted to the crusty diction of the Augustans. The strength of character that allowed him to be his own rebellious young man now solidified into dogmatic middle and old age. He was both pampered (by women) and pompous, a bit of a stuffed-shirt in fact. If he lost his Platonism, Coleridge's philosophising was either never absorbed or forgotten. He looked like a yokel, a hill farmer or shepherd, dressed in old bucolic clothes with a rugged and prematurely aged face even when young (a stranger who shared a coach with him thought he was sixty when he was still only thirty-six).

By 1808, then aged thirty-eight, his old left-wing political opinions (picked up from Revolutionary France and, more briefly, Godwin) were gone. We can read this in his *Tract on the Convention of Cintra* (1809). The future Duke of Wellington had been charged with driving the French out of Portugal. All was going well until the War Office appointed Hew Dalrymple, an elderly General, in his place. Dalrymple - unbelievably - not only allowed the defeated French Army to march out fully armed and with all its equipment but ordered the Royal Navy to take it home to France. Wordsworth's pamphlet expressed his and the whole country's "rage and indignation" as well as his own political opinions. "The true welfare of Britain is best promoted by the independence, freedom and honour of other nations."The nation state is the basis of all liberty and the War was therefore a moral enterprise to set free those countries which the French were subjugating.

The rest of his life seems fairly humdrum, at least outwardly, though every year he went on a summer tour. In 1829, when he was nearly sixty, he was in Ireland. One day he boasted he'd put in seventeen hours, from five in the morning to ten at night, climbed up (and then down) three mountains totalling six and a half thousand feet, walked two hours on the flat, rode for ten miles and then rode a second time for an hour and a half and all on "nothing but a poor breakfast of spongy bread without eggs and one crust of the same quality, and drank milk during the whole day".

Wordsworth always seems to have needed women around him. Isabella Fenwick was the last: a woman of private means with a house in Bath who took a cottage in Grasmere to be near him when he was about sixty-five and she was fifty. They even travelled together - he showed her his old College in Cambridge and took her to Durham when he received his honorary degree (DCL - Doctor of Common Law). In 1843 she persuaded him to tell her what he remembered about the origins some of his early poems and the reasons for writing them. Her jottings - the

IF Notes - are still studied though by the time she wrote them Wordsworth's boyhood, when he sank into the landscape and became part of nature, was half a century in the past.

Miss Fenwick also persuaded him to let his daughter, Dora, marry. Dora was then thirty-seven. Edward Quillinan (1791-1851) was born in Oporto where his Irish father was a wine merchant (his mother was Irish too). For a time he served with the 3rd Dragoon Guards in the Peninsular war. He was a poet and novelist but also semi-penniless with only his officer's half pay as a regular income. Dora died six years later, leaving Wordsworth once again devastated.

Industrialism's warping effect on people upset him, as did the ugliness it spawned, but he was also a prototype Nimby - not in my back yard - and in 1844 he campaigned to keep the railway out of the Lake District, and this after publishing several editions of his *Guide to the Lakes*. (According to Matthew Arnold, a clergyman once asked him had he written anything else.) In effect he campaigned to keep out the common folk - millhands from Lancashire (what did they know of beauty?) - the kind of people he'd earlier championed. He wrote a sonnet - *Suggested by the Proposed Kendal and Windermere Railway*:

And is no nook of English ground secure
From rash assault?

In spite of all this he proposed that the Lake District become "a sort of national property, in which every man has a right and an interest who has an eye to perceive and a heart to enjoy". The whole area became a National Park in 1951, though not restricted to those with eyes and hearts to see and perceive.

By the 1840s he needed a job. He wrote a rather grovelling letter to the Earl of Lonsdale and was given the Stamp Distributorship for Westmorland (and later parts of Lancashire and Cumberland). The Government collected some taxes through stamps which were sold by sub-distributors - shopkeepers very often - and fixed on legal documents, insurance policies, wills, even pamphlets. The Distributor stocked them in bulk, distributed them and collected the cash. Wordsworth kept stamps and cash in a great iron chest: eighteen thousand pounds, mainly in Scottish notes, at one time - over two million in today's money.

He was Lord Lonsdale's agent in the 1818 General Election. Lord Lowther and Colonel Lowther, sons of the Earl, were the Tory candidates and Westmorland's outgoing MPs. The Lonsdales owned all the Rotten Boroughs in the area but this time the election was contested. Henry Brougham (pronounced "broom") stood in the Whig interest. Brougham was a local boy and one of the founders of the *Edinburgh Review*, a magazine which began its criticism of Wordsworth's *The Excursion* with "This will never do". (The review of *The White Doe of Rylstone* began: "This, we think, has the merit of being the very worst poem we ever saw imprinted in a quarto volume.") Wordsworth didn't come out of it well - spying on lawyers in Kendal, identifying voters who could be bribed. He also seems to have been involved in selling plots of Lowther land: freeholders had a vote but there was no secret ballot and men with power knew how the lower orders voted. Some of his own family benefited apparently. As a civil servant - Stamp Distributor - all this was illegal.

The Wordsworths had five children but only two outlived them. After six years, the family left Dove Cottage because it was too small (de Quincey took it over for some time) and moved to Allan Bank, a new house outside the village, where the chimney smoked so badly they couldn't see across the room and newly washed plates blackened with soot. From there they went to the Parsonage, next to the church, on land so waterlogged and poorly drained that in bad weather their ground floor flooded. (Two of their five children died there in the same year, 1812: Catherine, three years old, and Thomas, aged six.) Rydal Mount, their final house, was bigger (a small mansion) on higher ground, set in four acres, with views as far as Windermere. He rented as he did all their houses and always bought second hand furniture. Here they were on the fringe of the county set and moved up a notch on the social scale.

Did his early poetry change society? de Quincey asked. "Up to 1820 the name of Wordsworth was trampled underfoot: from 1820 to 1830 it was militant: from 1830 to 1835 it has been triumphant". And in the end he did have friends in literary and other high places: he was Poet Laureate because the Prime Minister, Robert Peel, begged him to accept. In 1819 he became a Justice of the Peace. At the age of seventy-two he was given a Civil List Pension of £300 a year and he gave up the stamps.

Tourists gathered at his gate to stare. Dr Thomas Arnold, the muscular Christian headmaster of Rugby School bought a plot of land and built a second home, partly designed by Wordsworth, at Fox How to be near him. Wordsworth complained he saw little of the headmaster because of the swarms of children, one of whom was Matthew, the future sweetness and light Hellenist. Wordsworth was famous but unread in parts of the Lake Country: famous and read among the London elite: read and mocked by the *Edinburgh Review*.

John, his oldest son, was ordained: the Earl of Lonsdale gave him a living in the Lake District. Willy, the youngest, seems to have been unteachably dim-witted (expelled from Charterhouse after a year for idleness) and ended up taking over his father's stamp distributorship. The two of them left Wordsworth descendants as did his French daughter, Caroline. His wife, Mary, outlived him by eight years.

Whether in the end he believed in heaven is impossible to know. However, as he lay dying his wife told him he'd soon be with their daughter, Dora, whom he'd loved better than the rest. As his niece drew open the curtains the next morning he asked: "Is that Dora?"

CHAPTER III

Coleridge: "A Hunger for Eternity"

Your blessedness is not where most of you seek it, in things below you. How can that be? It must be a higher good to make you happy.

I may not hope from outward forms to win
The passion and the life, whose fountains are within.

S T COLERIDGE

In the early 19th century, a Dr Gillman and his wife looked after Coleridge at their house in Highgate on the northern hills above London. Carlyle called the summit "a waving blooming country of the brightest green." You looked down on London in the valley through an "olive-tinted haze". Coleridge's room was upstairs at the back with the best view of the garden, and the gardens of other tree-hidden houses. "The good man," Carlyle wrote, "he was now getting old, towards sixty perhaps; and gave you the idea of a life that had been full of sufferings; a life heavy-laden, half-vanquished, still swimming painfully in seas of manifold physical and other bewilderment. ... The deep eyes, of a light hazel, were as full of sorrow as of inspiration; confused pain looked mildly from them, as in a kind of mild astonishment.*"

But Coleridge also had, as Lamb put it, "a hunger for eternity". He wanted, in fact, to make personal contact with God. I'm not sure he ever really did - although one evening in Malta he noticed the "moon dim-glimmering thro' the dewy window-pane"*. It was trying, he believed, to open up a way for the eternity which was always hidden inside him to break surface and become consciously known. Why no contact? For one thing Coleridge was a thinker who could never stop thinking - and experience can only come when thought stops.

Mill called him one of the "seminal minds of his generation" and Wordsworth said he was the author of a whole string of "grand central truths". With Wordsworth he boosted - launched, even - the Romantic Movement in England, helped to temper English Empiricism, was at the bottom of American Transcendentalism and possibly also Pragmatism (via John Dewey). He influenced Christian Socialism, modernised literary criticism, rehabilitated Hamlet, and changed the way Shakespeare is staged (though he stole some ideas from Schelling). Coleridge also brought German Idealism to Britain - it was, for example, the main school of thought in English and Scottish universities until, overnight around 1900, Bertrand Russell replaced it with analytic philosophy.

How can mankind communicate with a wholly-other supernatural Being? To begin with, people can't have traits which are alien to their creator. Just as we need to be fulfilled through love and companionship, so does the Absolute. At the level of deity, that can happen only within a triune God - Father, Logos, Spirit. If we have a personality, the Trinity must have some Absolute version of the same - something which Coleridge called Personeity. Personeity and personality can, however dimly, make contact - and, at its strongest, you have the mystic vision.

His was a highly abstract concept of Christianity with the Logos (Reason, Intelligence) in place of miracles and a manger. The Logos holds the eternal Ideas which are also lodged in the human mind, in a watered down form but translucent enough to give us glimpses of eternity. The Logos is also the God within. Its presence sets us apart from the rest of creation and so lets us see things objectively, from the outside: if the mind were merely matter we couldn't do so.

He found the final part of the answer in aspects of German Idealism which he made his own. Idealism - crudely - favours mind over matter, the spiritual over the secular, tries to fit the finite into eternity.

He didn't always agree with Kant: if I understand him correctly, Coleridge argued that if we live in a mind-made world, as Kant claimed, then eternity and the divine must be just as real as space and time, causation or upside down and sideways.

Idealism also helped him tackle the mind/matter conundrum. Which is primary? The answer I think he got from Schelling*. Matter is Mind which is still asleep, ready to be woken. Both man's mind and nature's are in God and are, presumably, one and the same.

But especially and essentially he took the ideas of Reason/Understanding from Kant and Imagination/Fancy from Schelling.

What we call reason, Coleridge called Understanding. Reason, for him, is a conduit through which the Logos makes direct contact with the human mind. Through this intuitive channel each lesser mind can speak to the Greater, the source of all being. Reason is the two-way "ladder pitched betwixt Heaven and Charing Cross".

Primary Imagination* is the equivalent of Reason in art and science - a conduit along which the Logos carries raw ideas straight from the store house in eternity into our minds. (Secondary Imagination then works on them.) Imagination (or *esemplastic power*) is "the repetition in the finite mind of the eternal act of creation in the infinite I Am … art, science, philosophy are all aspects of this infinite creativity." We're only fully alive when we're aware of these things but "only the Fewest among the Few live in their Light". (Fancy is little more than memory - it recalls what's already been created but can't break it down to make something new.)

Coleridge always thought in dichotomies or binaries and in this way paired civilisation and culture. Civilisation is the hardware - science, trade, commerce, money-making - on which our spiritual and cultural software rests. Locke's materialist philosophy was good at making the hardware but at the same time harmed society's culture and spirituality. Society had become "varnished rather than polished - perilously over-civilised, most piteably uncultivated". The Age of Reason had abandoned the "platonic spirit of old England".

Although creativity is divine, I suspect Coleridge also knew that the mind has to be pre-stocked with the kind of knowledge which broadens and deepens it. Schools are the obvious places but who should in be charge? Schoolmasters? The clergy? Neither. Schools should be run by the Clerisy, a word Coleridge coined. It means the learned guardians, expanders, and passers-on of culture - scholars, scientists, writers, priests, philosophers - Burkean intermediaries between the gone and the yet to be.

As we've seen, Newman's concept of the illuminated mind began with Coleridge - a man who never seemed to benefit from it. Did he ever see life steadily and see it whole? He was not so much filled with Hellenic sweetness and light as with Germanic sourness and gloom? He was, in fact, driven by a compulsion to merge the best ideas in philosophy into a single system but he was so unsystematic that his ideas are half-lost in an immense welter of words scattered through books, magazines, letters, lectures, speeches, table talk, marginalia and notes for a never published *Magnum Opus*. That being so, I can't vouch for total accuracy of this account of Coleridge's thought.

CHAPTER IV

Inventing Oblong Wheels

Platonism fits the West best because the mind behind it was also the mind behind the wider secular culture but by the 1920s it had almost completely vanished as Christianity weakened and materialism took over. Yet an interest in mysticism (without Plato) lingered on for about forty years, starting in the 1950s, ending in a row of reinvented wheels which didn't quite fit the wagon. The new mysticism fell into four groups: scientific research, psychedelic drugs, Eastern, and the odd lone seeker or researcher.

Science began to research mysticism, minus Plato, in the 1890s and early 1900s. William James to begin with, then Edwin Diller Starbuck (1866-1947) and James Henry Leuba (1868-1946) (who wanted to show, I think, that mysticism is psychological and not spiritual). All used the questionnaire method which Inge disliked: some won't answer, some won't tell the truth, some like answering and they aren't the ones you want to hear from.

In 1969 Sir Alister Hardy* set up his Religious Experience Unit in what became Harris Manchester College, Oxford. (Now it's the Alister Hardy Research Centre in the University of Wales, Lampeter.) The West was in decay from the lack of a spiritual element and he hoped to find a way to reverse the decline. The spiritual is normal and necessary but materialism was blocking it. That "unappeased religious desire" needed the support of a spiritual philosophy which, in turn, doesn't contradict science and the Theory of Evolution. Platonism, in other words, was what he was looking for yet in *The Spiritual Nature of Man* (1979) neither Plato nor Plotinus nor any in the long list of their followers is mentioned. (Socrates appears because of his daemon.)

Hardy says the mystical experience gives us a "sense of joy, peace, security, awe, reverence, and wonder; feelings of exaltation and ecstasy, of harmony and unity, of hope and fulfilment". And, he adds, a sense of "timelessness .. of presence .. of purpose .. of prayer answered in events". It was not, however, a contact with the "supernatural", a word he shied away from preferring "para-physical" - above the physical, presumably, but not above nature. Is any of this so strange? he also asked. Can anything be stranger than the fact of consciousness itself? How matter can generate non-matter is one of the great unresolved riddles of science.

Fifteen percent of the four thousand people who wrote to Hardy's research unit in the 1970s thought their childhood experiences of the transcendent were of lifelong importance. Surveys carried out by the National Opinion Poll on behalf of two of Hardy's assistants showed that forty-one percent of females and thirty-one percent of males had had mystical experiences which, if accurate, is enough for a Platonist revival.

Hardy met Walter Pahnke (1931-1971) in Baltimore in 1968. Pahnke had degrees in theology, medicine, and psychiatry - specifically to qualify him (Hardy suggests) to study drugs *and* mysticism. In 1962 he carried out the Good Friday Experiment to see if psilocybin could induce genuine mystical experiences in ten students. It did for nine of them, Pahnke claimed. (Timothy Leary was one of his thesis supervisors: Leary, deep into psychedelic drugs and the counterculture of the 1960s, was famous for the escapist catchphrase "turn on, tune in, drop out".) "Thus at long last," Pahnke wrote, "research into mysticism need no longer be limited to the scholarly scrutiny of various devotional or metaphysical documents left behind by such historic personages as Shankara, Plotinus, Meister Eckhart, William Blake and Teresa of Avila. Persons can be studied extensively both before and after the experience of mystical consciousness in controlled settings". He drowned while scuba diving off the coast of Maine.

For a time in Baltimore Panhke also worked with Stanislav Grof, the transpersonal psychologist, who went on in the 1980s to drug volunteer guinea-pigs with LSD. He called the drug "an amplifier, or catalyst, of mental processes which facilitate the emergence of unconscious material from different levels of the human psyche". By then a new word had also been invented - *entheogen* (from the Greek for "god-created-within") - for any drug which induced "non-ordinary states of consciousness". Grof made up his own word - holotropic: "moving towards wholeness". This movement was caused by "holotropic breath work" - hyperventilating until the brain is nearly completely starved of oxygen and the body is close to death.

Meanwhile, more conventional psychologists mostly kept away from a subject that wasn't career furthering. Those who took an interest effectively unwove the rainbow as Keats feared. "Fischer (1971) distinguishes the ergotropic (increased arousal) from the trophotropic (decreased arousal); elsewhere green and mature (Levin & Steele, 2005) or hyper versus hypo states have also been described (McCraty et al., 2009). Internal-to-internal entrainment is commonly observed in meditating subjects where, for example, heart rate and respiration may coordinate or even interact with brain-wave frequency. Similarly, ideas of neural synchronisation (harmony) and coherence (stability) in low-amplitude alpha and theta bands may characterise integrated functioning and quieten cognitive chatter (Hebert et al., 2005)." (Examples from Ray McBride, *the Psychologist* (2014).)

In the 1970s and '80s a few people in America were predicting a paradigm shift which would Easternise and feminise the West. It had already begun with the fusion, as they saw it, of mysticism and quantum physics. Books about the new physics and mysticism came out year by year. Fritjof Capra's *The Tao of Physics* began it all and over the next few years he wrote *The Turning Point* and *Uncommon Wisdom*. There was also Michael Talbot's *Mysticism and the New Physics* and Gary Zukav's *The Dancing Wu Li Masters* - among many others.

Alan Watts* (1915-1973) regarded Eastern mysticism as the way to renew a flagging Western civilisation: *The Way of Zen* (1957), in fact, was a best seller in the swinging psychedelic '60s among young people looking for what had been lost and never since found. His answer was the personal experience of God which reveals there is no personality, only a cosmic oneness. Meanwhile the religious void, he said, was filled with everything from drunkenness to state-worship. Later in the book he offers another answer: "It is not too much to predict that the next great step in Christian theology will be due, in part, to the absorption of Hinduism, Buddhism, Taoism, and, perhaps, Sufism, all of which are profoundly mystical religions." Curiously, Platonism *is* mentioned - in this very same paragraph - but only because Origen, St Clement and St Augustine followed it.

Yoga and Zen also had followings for a time. Yoga (yoke - tethering the mind to eternity) seems to have had several purposes - relaxation, easing life's pain, fitness and the widening of consciousness to merge with the whole. *Samadhi* (*satori* in Zen) was the end point - mind yoked to the All. Zen meant, in the main, *zazen* or sitting, mind stilling - the goal being union with the Buddha-nature or just peace descending. Both clearly have the same source as Platonism, made different by culture, and more systematised. Students in The Academy in Plato's own day practised mind-stilling exercises. In the *Phaedo*, Socrates advises his friends to expand their minds to take in the whole cosmos. "Become Cosmos" could have been the motto of the first Academy: the soul must lift itself above the worldly to contemplate the divine. Greek Orthodoxy is the most Platonic of the Christian churches and its monks to this day practise *hesychasm* or the way of stillness. The Jesus Prayer is their mantra.

Then there were the lone seekers and researchers such as Aldous Huxley* and Marghanita Laski. Huxley was best known at one time for his experiments with drug induced altered states. *The Doors of Perception* (about mescalin) came out in 1954. He had no experience of mysticism himself but mescalin he hoped would open the way for him. He thought it did: the Beatific Vision, he called it. Laski - who reviewed his book - didn't believe it. She began with duration. Ecstatic moments, as she called them, are just that: moments - seconds long most usually. Half an hour is a very long time, and also very, very rare. What she calls the "afterglow" can last as long, or longer, but not the experience itself. The drugged state, on the other hand, can last for hours. Also, the ecstatic mood can change from "dread to delight" but never "delight to dread" as it can with drugs. The ecstatic moment is timeless but the spaced out are still aware of time, they just don't care about it. (Laski concedes that Huxley spoke of "timeless bliss" but points out he was versed in the vocabulary of mysticism.)

What would normally be regarded as non-triggers can trigger the drugged: Huxley was switched on by his trousers, for example. She's wrong however in scorning walls. Huxley wrote about a "blank but unforgettably beautiful" stucco'd wall, "empty but charged with all the meaning and mystery of existence." And Laski herself, in a footnote, mentions da Vinci's advice to painters to look for signs of divinity in damp walls. Things "glowed" for Huxley with bright colours which gave them a profound significance. He describes a deckchair "with stripes of deep but glowing indigo alternated with stripes of iridescence so intensely bright that they could not be made of anything but blue fire".

Huxley was wrong about drugs and divinity but he did believe you can judge the quality of a society by how it helps people grow "towards the goal of human existence" - which is, quite simply, a meeting with the divine. But, in spite of its importance, the West had turned away from the spiritual towards the material. Writing in 1946, he also stressed what happened without it - nationalism, statism, revolutionism and "state- worship, boss-worship". The cause of the decline, Huxley thought, was Christianity's homing in too hard on history - what happened in Galilee and Judea in the 1st century - and an "undervaluation of the everlasting, timeless fact of eternity".

Huxley's *Perennial Philosophy* (1944) is an overview of mysticism illustrated by quotations from most of the world's esoteric traditions. Nearly forty percent of the books in the bibliography are about Eastern mysticism and Plato is quoted only once: "We are saved, we are liberated and enlightened ... by returning to our eternal Ground". Huxley adds: "Plato speaks in the same sense when he says, in the *Republic,* that "the virtue of wisdom more than anything else contains a divine element which always remains." Huxley also goes on to say that Plato in the *Theaetetus* tells us that to become God-like you must know God, "identify ourselves with the divine element which in fact constitutes our essential nature".

Marghanita Laski (1915-1988) knew nothing about Platonism and at times she also seemed to confuse mysticism with bouts of extreme happiness, which she called ecstasies. She really did reinvent the wheel: she researched the entire subject from scratch and wrote up her findings in two books: *Ecstasy* (1961) and *Everyday Ecstasy* (1980). She read English in Oxford in the 1930s, but an Oxford perhaps more like *Brideshead Revisited* than the city of Ruskin, Jowett, Pater or Inge. Laski never seems to have heard of Caroline Spurgeon (1869-1942) who wrote *Mysticism and English Literature* (1913), perhaps the best book on Plato and English poetry ever written. She did however know the work of Evelyn Underhill whose most famous book, *Mysticism* (1911), is still read and in which she seriously underestimates Plato and Wordsworth (she "detected indications of the illuminative life" in them). Laski had also read Inge's *Christian Mysticism* but seemed unaware of the Christian Platonism which he thought could save the West. Ruskin is missing entirely.

Laski was an atheist, journalist, novelist and the most prolific contributor ever to the *Oxford English Dictionary* - a quarter of a million slips. She was also a TV panellist, appearing in *The Brains Trust* in the 1950s, *What's My Line* ('50s into the '60s), and *Any Questions* also in the 1960s. She never had an ecstatic experience herself although she was sometimes moved by old fabrics, ceramics and jewellery. But she knew that ecstasies are good for you physically and mentally: they boost creativity and make the mind more complex. What's a good touchstone for proving the genuineness of an ecstatic moment? Out of her long list, the best is probably what she called "the test of benefit". It makes for a "well-lived day", a writer in the Hampstead Hills told her. She also quotes St Teresa of Avila: if the experience makes you bigger and better you can take it that it's the real thing.

Her first book hinged on a questionnaire. "Do you know a sensation of transcendent ecstasy?" If the answer was "yes", the follow-on questions were: "How would you describe it?" "What has induced it in you?" "How many times in your life have you felt it - in units, tens, hundred." "What is your religion or faith?" "Do you know a feeling of creative inspiration?" "Does it (inspiration, that is) seem to have anything in common with ecstasy?" "What is your profession?'"

Her first sample was very small: sixty-three adults who all lived in the Hampstead Hills, one of London's richest suburbs, and where she herself had a house. Nearly a third of her first sample were professional writers. Almost all the rest were from a similar background. Of the sixty-three all but two had experienced "transcendent ecstasy". That's around ninety-seven percent. Could it possibly be right? Or were those well-to-do people merely very happy every now and then?

Some time later, she posted a hundred copies of a doctored version of the questionnaire ("transcendent" became "unearthly") through letter boxes in a "working class district of London". A stamped addressed envelope was enclosed but no cash incentive. She was lucky to get eleven replies, particularly as ten of them said "no". Only one said "yes" - a middle-aged newspaper packer who'd left school at fifteen around the time of the Great War. The mystic experience wasn't ordinary happiness, he told her: it was brought on by "sunsets, beautiful music, scenery from heights, eg from Snowdon, Helvellyn, etc. Also masses of flowers." He'd experienced it dozens of times - it was "indescribable. Peace, accompanied by a little heavier breathing and sometimes a feeling of wanting to close my eyes and cry". As for changing him he said: "Not exactly changed but certainly strengthened my appreciation of life". He'd never read a book about mysticism and Rationalism was his religion.

Using answers to her questionnaire Laski graded ecstatic states as adamic, knowledge, unitive. Unitive is the classic end point of high level mysticism (in her second book she calls them "contact experiences"). Adamic was named after Adam and Eve and the Garden of Eden in all its purity, innocence and original kindness. The middle rung she called Knowledge because people who experience it learn something.

She also worked out that the experience can be triggered both inwardly or outwardly. She called them Intensity and Withdrawal ecstasies. The year before *Ecstasy* came out, however, W T Stace published two books in which they're called introvertive and extrovertive. Laski never knew about him.

Adamics, she tells us in her second book, favour three-legged stools, sandals, settles, herbal tea, peasant-woven wool, earthenware mugs, hand-dyed cotton, spades, discomfort, equality of outcome and communal eating. Adamics are young collectivists with a tendency to set up New Age or hippie or flower power communes. Even Jesus was an adamic advocate of hippie living, as was William Morris (1834-1896). Morris's utopian novel, *News from Nowhere* (1890), is about an adamic future, the Middle Ages with plumbing. Happiness has made everybody good looking. There are no schools, no schooling, no police, soldiers, or government. Food is plentiful and free, even in restaurants and guest houses. Work, which is carried out only by those who want to, is based on the Arts and Crafts ethos - the industrial cities have been razed, replaced by hamlets in the Greenwood.

Adamics, Laski tells us, put feeling before intellect while Knowledge types favour hierarchies and intellectual utopias such as Bacon's *New Atlantis*, Plato's *Republic* or More's *Utopia*. The Oxford and Cambridge colleges are, in fact, examples of knowledge-type communes, set up by academics in their more ecstatic moments, or so I believe Laski said.

CHAPTER V

An Abuse of Reason

Caught in that sensual music all neglect
Monuments of unaging intellect.

W B YEATS

Those who couple Rationalism with unbelief, or at any rate with a cold, critical temper, should be reminded of the essentially devout rationalism of the Cambridge Platonists, which arose as a protest against the materialism of Hobbes. The little group, of whom Whichcote, John Smith, Henry More and Cudworth were the most conspicuous, followed the Neoplatonists in exalting reason, while at the same time believing in a mystical illumination transcending the discursive reason which we use in judging of earthly things.

History seems to show us ... that the powers of evil have won their greatest triumphs by capturing the organisations which were formed to defeat them, and that when the Devil has changed the contents of the bottles he never alters the labels.

DEAN INGE

The rot set in with the Enlightenment which began in England after the Restoration in the late 17th century. In an Age of Reason *The Am* couldn't stand up to scrutiny (though *The Is* can). The path led from the Enlightenment, via British Empiricism and Continental Rationalism, through Kant and a peculiarly Germanic line of Idealist thought until it merged in the 20th century with Existentialism, the French New Left, Marxism and Cultural Marxism and came out as Post-Modernist Neo-Marxism. On the way it obliterated Platonism and badly damaged

Christianity. Reason turned on reason then used reason to promote irrationality. The West became too materialist and therefore unbalanced.

Essentially, I'd argue, reason destroyed belief in the transcendent, allowing irrational bitterness filled the hole. (Oddly enough in the 1730s George Berkeley, like Eliot's Tiresias, "perceived the scene and foretold the rest"*.)

Jean-Jacques Rousseau (1712-1778) was the first to attack the Enlightenment. Civilisation is corrupt because it's based on reason which pushed the noble savage away from a natural life of passion and instinct into hierarchical societies. Culture led to "luxury, learning and moral decay". Reason is the "original sin" which changed human nature itself, giving rise to alpha males who dominate and oppress. Oppressors work to keep things as they are but Europe needed a revolution to rid itself of civilisation. If you can't go back to Eden, then at least settle for tribalism - or utter and complete collectivism where the individual counts for nothing and the whole counts for all, where everything is based on passion, feelings, emotion and the banishment of reason. You'll also need a state religion to enforce order and stability by killing anybody not outwardly conforming: there'll be no room for individuality - individuals, on the contrary, will devote their lives, bodies and minds to the collective. A great Leader, who understands the General Will, is to have powers of life and death. You will be "forced to be free" - until the Leader thinks it time to kill you.

But the period between 1780/1815, when Germany took over as the major Western philosophical nation, was the real turning point. In *Explaining Post-Modernism* (2017) Stephen Hicks argues that the Germans had long been doubtful about the Enlightenment - it damaged religion, tradition, the collective and induced selfishness. It was reductionist and mechanistic - scaling down passion, creativity, free will. What about community, self-sacrifice, duty?

The Anglo-Irish Berkeley and the Scottish Hume were the immediate catalysts. George Berkeley (1685-1753) was an immaterialist* who argued that the material world is held in God's mind. *Esse est percipi*: to be is to be seen. Things exist only when they're noticed, held in a consciousness, but God holds the cosmos in his Mind and is aware of everything all the time.

David Hume (1711-1776) agreed that that we live in a mind-made world but that mind is yours, even though you have no self and are just a bundle of random impressions. His greatest insight? "Reason is passion's slave", or most beliefs are rationalised emotion. More seriously, he got rid of both God (there are no measurable facts proving his existence) and science (there's no proof that one thing causes another).

Emmanuel Kant (1724-1804) had to counter these last two arguments both to clear a way for belief in God (by getting rid of pure reason) and to save science (by restoring cause and effect as facts). People sit around thinking deep thoughts about philosophy but never examine the thing they're thinking with. What are the limits of the mind? To begin with, the brain makes the world we live in*. Imagine your brain is a digital camera set to black and white: photons - data - from the colourful outer world pass through the eye-lens and then through a processor which makes your cosmos monochrome. The brain is, in fact, like a black box crammed with electronics. Five sensors gather data which are passed through twelve processors, called the Categories two of which create a sense of space and time while a third makes cause and effect a reality in the only world you can know. This inner space Kant called phenomenon: the outer is noumenon - utterly unknowable and so out of bounds to pure reason. This means that God's existence can be neither proved nor disproved, thus opening the way for belief through faith. Practical reason, however, tells us that some things are universal - a sense of duty and morality, for example - so belief in a deity is not wholly unthinkable.

But Kant, I suspect, was an Incomplete, born without the 13th Category - if you can sense eternity, then eternity in your self-made cosmos must be as real as space, time, up, down and sideways, or causality., as I believe Coleridge pointed out.

Like his master Rousseau, Kant was an extreme collectivist who'd figured out nature's plan - to evolve a fully perfected human species with no room for the individual. It's right that you should suffer because you were born sinful and chose reason over the instincts and now your desires run amok. Your freedom therefore is based on sin. Force is the only way to straighten the "crooked timber of mankind" - the force of duty, to begin with: you have a duty to actualise yourself in order to evolve the species through morality. A strong leader is also needed to force you to obey the General Will. War, too, speeds up evolution and is therefore good. Peace is bad but all will end in utopia - a peaceful world of "complete moral development".

Georg Wilhelm Friedrich Hegel (1770-1831) upended Kant and turned his theory inside out - literally: there is no noumenon because the entire cosmos is phenomenon. Your mind isn't claustrophobically encased in a skull - it's more like a cell in a universal Geist or Spirit which is evolving, with your help, to complete self-knowledge through a dialectical clash of contradictions - the first of which, if I understand it, was matter itself.

We also belong to the State which, being more highly developed, is closer to fully evolved divinity and so has to be obeyed and even worshipped. The State is part of the Absolute and so freedom is through total submission to it. "The State is the Divine Idea as it exists on Earth."

The Geist evolves dialectically in three-step phases - thesis, antithesis, synthesis. Pre-Socratic Greeks had a certain level of consciousness (thesis): Socrates was more highly evolved (antithesis) and so created a synthesis resulting in a higher level of consciousness: but this new level was also a thesis waiting for Plato's antithesis to expand awareness yet again - and so it has gone on down the ages, though it may have stalled today.

Karl Marx (1818-1883) was an Hegelian but instead of being an Idealist he was a Dialectical Materialist: society - not a Geist - is working its way through inner contradictions and three-step phases - Feudal/Capitalist/Communist - to an earthly paradise of perfected people who will "hunt in the morning, fish in the afternoon, rear cattle in the evening, criticise after dinner" with no need of laws or governments. First however a revolution will overthrow capitalism and the class system along with the rich and materially successful - a final synthesis which never again will be a thesis: evolution will be complete, history ended.

In *Glittering Images* (2012), Camille Paglia points out some of Marxism's limitations: it "lacks a metaphysics - that is, an investigation of man's relationship to the universe, including nature. Marxism also lacks a psychology: it believes that human beings are motivated only by material needs and desires. Marxism cannot account for the infinite refractions of human consciousness, aspirations, and achievement." In other words, it's single-stranded in a multi-stranded world. Worse, any hint of transcendence is also missing, leaving a gaping void which the human need for religion can fill with almost anything, and does.

Friedrich Nietzsche (1844-1900) was, I think, a near-miss Platonist, an Almost-Complete, yet he too condemned reason for causing the fall of mankind and, very oddly, corrupting philosophy. Consciousness is the "weakest and most fallible organ". People aren't driven by facts or reason but by the distorting tricks of language, by damaged psychologies, by badly thought through cultures, and by resentment. The intellect is puny, ruled by forces it can't understand or control and so uses reason to hide from the world's savagery. Religion and morals are con tricks of the weak and craven to cow the strong. But all is not lost - soon a race of superior people will lift themselves above the fate of humanity into a higher state of being: the Overmen, the Supermen, who will be guided by instincts so deep they'll be in touch with ultimate reality. Socrates was wrong because he raised reason (Apollo) above the passions and instincts (Dionysus).

Yet, another part of Nietzsche's mind was half-way Ruskinian: the meaning of life is to be found only through art, music and tragedy, in depths beyond the reach of reason. Wisdom, which is deeper than good and evil, comes when art shuts down the self. Sensitivity to the invisible is an instinct and so should be respected: it can turn the mystic into a Superman particularly if he uses his "will to power" to do what Plato advised - control the appetites and harmonise the soul.

In *Human, All Too Human,* first written in the 1870s, Nietzsche said he regretted the loss of great art such as that of Dante, Raphael, Michelangelo and the Gothic Cathedrals. It was great, he recognised, because it was based on spiritual and religious beliefs even if those beliefs were wrong - made, in fact, by "the glorifiers of the religious and philosophical errors of mankind". If the decline in the spiritual goes on, he went on, there will never again be such great art because "it presupposes not only a cosmic but a metaphysical significance".

Earlier in the same book he tells us that metaphysics and the thinking man don't fit together but the thinker still feels the pull of the spiritual. When he becomes aware of it "he feels a profound stab in the heart and sighs for the man who will lead him

back to his lost love, whether she be called religion or metaphysics. It is in such moments", he adds, "that his intellectual probity
is put to the test." By the end of the 19th century, Christianity
was slipping away into nihilism - that is, into no-belief rather
than disbelief - and resentment threatened to destroy the entire
West

Yet, also from the same book, it's plain that Nietzsche didn't
associate beauty with eternity. "Beauty entered this system only
incidentally, without essentially encroaching upon the fundamental sense of the uncanny and exalted, of consecration by
magic and the proximity of the divine." He adds: "at most beauty
mitigated the *dread*".

Nietzsche also gave us two useful insights: resentment is
the default position of most of mankind and getting rid of the
spiritual was always going to end in trouble.

Early 20th century Continental philosophy took two routes:
Existentialism and Cultural Marxism. Both were German
although Cultural Marxism (or the Frankfurt School) began
with Gramsci's Cultural Hegemony which planned to by-pass
the proletariat, who'd let Marx down by failing to revolt in the
Great War, by colonising the minds of the future ruling class
with a destructive ideology, strategy and tactics instead.

Martin Heidegger (1889-1976) also thought that reason
is trivial and that ideas and words block the way to reality. He
too dismissed Socrates because Greek reason and questioning
had drained the West of life and left people inauthentic, adrift
from what they should be and, because of that, devoid of any
sense of meaning.

Heidegger, as I understand it, was both an Existentialist
and a Phenomenologist - that is, a philosopher who studied
his own mind, or Kant's phenomenon. Go inside and view
your feelings - boredom, fear, guilt, dread. Start with boredom
and be bored until you're totally detached from everything.
This makes you anxious and afraid, full of dread, because your

sense of individuality has been lost. Accept it, fill yourself with dread, sink and collapse into it because it paves the way to the final solution to the problem of the mystery of life. This sense of dissolving is a "foretaste of death" and shows that Ultimate Being and Nothingness are one and the same - an everlasting, bottomless void.

Sōtō Zen does something similar: the would-be *rōshi* sits silently watching images and thoughts aimlessly appearing and passing through his mind until it shuts down and he senses eternity or achieves *satori*. I wonder if this wasn't what Heidegger was up but instead of the beatific vision he saw only the horror of his own mind?

French philosophers and novelists like Sartre and Camus then took up Existentialism, which had quite a vogue among young men in polo-necked sweaters in the 1950s (the era of kitchen sink dramas). Its slogan - *existence precedes essence* - sums it up: there is no *Is* - only alienation, dread, absurdity and pitiful creatures abandoned in a Godless cosmos.

Roger Scruton describes some of the French New Left in *Fools, Frauds and Firebrands* (2015): Lyotard, Foucault, Derrida, Althusser, Deleuse, Lacan. "A deep disappointment with reality and a desire to tear it down in the name of Utopia has been the default position of left-wing thinking in France from the Jacobins to the present day." Their problem? Loss of religion. Their tactic? Talk gibberish about ideas of "staggering imbecility" to keep out reason. The West was to rot from the head down so they targeted universities.

Cultural Marxism met the New Left in post-War American universities. In the 1960s, the Cultural Marxist, Herbert Marcuse (1898-1979), having fled the Nazis in the 1930s, was still teaching when the Boomers reached college age. The ideas in his *Eros and Civilization, One-Dimensional Man* and *The Aesthetic Dimension* effectively colonised enough minds to make history and then the New Left came along to join in.

Long before then, however, Adorno and Horkheimer, fellow members of the Frankfurt School, had already foretold the fate of the West in *Dialectic of Enlightenment* (1944). The West would fall in three stages:

Exhaustion of art and culture:

Universal childishness, infantilism and tantrums:

A new ideology finally leaving the West in ruins.

Now there's a rash of recently invented faculties which, essentially, teach resentment and stoke unappeasable rage and self-pity. Almost all these "studies" are collectivist - the group is primary - and either dismiss or misuse reason: critical race theory, identity politics, postcolonial studies, women's and trans-gender studies, de-colonialism, ethnic studies, indigenous/settler colonialism studies, disability studies, gender and sexuality studies, transnational studies, the patriarchy, toxic masculinity, white privilege and fragility, intersectionality, victimhood. Empirical evidence isn't proof, logical proof is theoretical, reason is artificial and dehumanising, reason is too subjective to understand reality, words and ideas block the way to the destruction of the West so unmask or deconstruct them. If there's no reason, then reasoned argument is uncalled for and unwanted and then gets in the way and should be banned.

CHAPTER VI

The Arts: "A Kind of Anxiety"

Ruskin's great discovery was the close connection of the decay of art with faulty social arrangements. Ugliness in the works of man is a symptom of disease in the State. This was Ruskin's conviction, and we may call it his discovery.

As soon as the seen and unseen worlds fall apart and lose connection with each other, both are dead. Such a severance at once cuts the nerve which makes the Platonist a poet. So long as the angels of thought and vision can pass freely up and down the ladder which leuds from earth to heaven, poetry of the highest kind is implicit in Platonism, whether it finds utterance or not; but so soon as God is banished from earth, and the beauty of form and colour from heaven, both are surrendered to the formless infinite which for Plato and his disciples is the privation of goodness and reality.

Modernism prides itself on a repudiation of all traditions and all accepted canons of beauty.

But several of the arts seem to have already reached their perfection, and then "stopped", as Aristotle says. We can hardly imagine that there will ever be greater sculptors than Pheidias, greater painters than Raphael and Rembrandt,

To repeat: in the Platonic scheme of things, the arts have to do
two things - introduce us the eternal and offer us novel insights
into the human psyche. To do so they have to obey the rules
governing their natures. They work best in a cohesive society,
not one tribalised and fragmented. Above all a sense of some
kind of transcendence has to be there, in the background perhaps but not entirely absent. In return they reveal at a glance
the health of a country - ugly, discordant societies make broken
art, while broken art works in a positive feedback loop making
things worse.

The arts in the West are both failing and revealing just how
broken this society has become, although it's been a century
long descent. Matthew Arnold, for example, wanted to turn
poetry into a religion to fill the spiritual void left by collapsing
Christianity. In his essay, *The Study of Poetry* (1888), he argues
that we need it "to interpret life for us, to console us, to sustain
us. Most of what now passes for religion and philosophy will be
replaced by poetry". In fact "The strongest part of our religion
today is its unconscious poetry." Without poetry, even science
will be incomplete.

But great poetry, Arnold also said, is not made in isolation:
the man and the moment must come together because the well-
read minds of individuals aren't enough if they live in sterile

times. Shakespeare was not a "deep reader" and Sophocles in any case had few books to read but the ages in which they lived were "permeated by fresh thought, intelligent and alive". In barren ages, the job of the critic is to replicate those rare periods, prime the times for greatness. The critic has to avoid polemics, politics, the controversial and become perfect "by making his mind dwell on what is excellent in itself, and the absolute beauty and fitness of things". He has "simply to know the best that is known and thought in the world, and by making this known, create a current of true and fresh ideas".

In 1893, five years after Arnold's warning and solution, Modernism began, fittingly, with Munch's *Scream*. Quite a debut, but the painter says nothing deep about life or eternity, only about his own shortcomings and a society that had lost its way: art reflecting corrosion but unable to create anything to counteract it. Expressionism began in Germany in 1905, in what was once called the long Edwardian summer, yet it too displayed disturbed minds and a damaged society. Picasso painted *Les Demoiselles d'Avignon* two years later. If the human world is empty, broken and in pieces, then the artist should paint it that way: the form should be broken as well as the content. "Show, not tell." In 1917 Marcel Duchamp hung a urinal on a wall in an art exhibition (open to all who paid the fee) in New York. "I thought to discourage aesthetics," he said. "I threw the bottle rack and the urinal in their faces and now they admire them for their aesthetic beauty." Spengler, writing in 1918, said the newly established avant-garde was turning against its own society and tearing it apart. As for Dali's Post-War Surrealism - if there's no objective truth, then paint the world as hallucination. Soon, Morris Weitz declared that art is whatever is called art. George Dickie added that art is what the art world says art is. Now art is anything that a self-styled artist does.

Cause and effect were known form the beginning. Alfred Noyes* (1880-1958) begins *Some Aspects of Modern Poetry* (1920) with art's essential roots: "But, inasmuch as we ourselves are part of this inscrutable universe, by opening within ourselves our own private wicket-gate into the Reality, of which we ourselves are part, it is possible for us to attain to certain forms of knowledge beyond the reach of inductive reason. All great art does that in its inspired moments."

He adds: "All great art reaches, in a flash, something of that universal knowledge which Plato … endeavoured to draw through the gate of the individual soul."

We're in danger of losing this "master-light", Noyes goes on, and so of losing the arts altogether. Many writers then living understood passion but few had any spiritual vision, unlike Wordsworth for whom "the visible universe was a perpetual shadowing forth of the invisible." Worse, "it has become the fashion to estimate a man's power in art and literature by his ability to suggest the utter futility of human effort, and the ultimate meaninglessness of the universe." The moderns, in fact, had "failed to do the work of natural development, failed to make their greater synthesis, not because they were too big for their age, but because their age was too big for them." Even in 1920, the true rebels were those who tried to keep alive the central truths of life and were forced to defend "lost causes against the intellectual mob that is incapable of understanding its own deeper loss."

Groupthink was in evidence long before the word was coined: "It is a strange spectacle this," Noyes wrote, "a hundred thousand rebels, each chained to the same comfortable peak, and all chanting in perfect unison exactly the same thing, a perennial song of hate against the things that are more excellent: criticism practically unanimous in applauding them: and each individual of the vast multitude believing himself to be entirely original, thinking for himself, and utterly alone."

Inge reviewed *Some Aspects of Modern Poetry* in the London *Evening Standard* in 1924: "Our young rebels declare that a painter need not know how to draw, and that poetry must "get rid of its music". Accordingly they produce pictures which suggest the handiwork of a very unpleasant child, and "free verse", which can be distinguished from sloppy prose, because it is cut up into uneven lengths. ... They form little coteries, praising each other, and all show a malignant desire to depreciate the great men of former generations, especially those of the latter half of the Nineteenth Century.... They chant in unison a hymn of hate against all things beautiful, noble, and of good report: and somehow they get themselves accepted as critics by editors who have no sympathy with revolution."

There was also, as Inge noted in his review, an unreasoning rage against the Victorians, a resentful rejection of all they'd done. Yet you need to know the past if you're ever going to make something both new and better. Forgetting the past is like losing your memory and you're the lesser for it. "Real newness never comes from hunting. It comes from within: and, for its expression, depends on the right use of a language that is already in existence."

A few Victorian modernist poets also knew what was happening to their civilisation and offered a way out. Ezra Pound (1885-1972) vilified the West - "an old bitch gone in the teeth ... a botched civilisation" - but he also quoted Stéphane Mallarmé* (1842-1898): we need to "purify the dialect of the tribe" in order to revive poetry until "change hath broken down/All things save beauty alone". Imagism, at least in Pound's mind, was an attempt to break free of space and time in order to reach a higher level of consciousness, propelled by the power of an image, unhindered by too many words. (Imagist poetry was based on a misunderstanding of haiku, about which not a lot was known in the early 20th century.)

T S Eliot (1888-1965) was a pin-stripe and spats man, a banker and a publisher yet *The Waste Land* (1921/22) is a lament for the decay of civilisation. Eliot was still non-Christian when he wrote it although the title is from the Arthurian cycle about the search for the Holy Grail which will cure the groin-hurt Fisher-King and bring the kingdom back to health. The land is wasted by spiritual, not material, poverty and the Holy Grail is spirituality itself, or perhaps even the mystic experience which, later in life, Eliot wanted to have but never found. The ending of *The Wasteland*, is bookish and unfelt - three words taken from the Sanskrit of the *Upanishads*: "give, sympathise, control". *The Four Quartets* (1935/42), like *The Scholar Gipsy*, is a quest poem. Unlike Arnold, Eliot knew what he was looking for - a sense of eternity - but not how to find it. He also had some idea of what it would be like: it was an insight into the singleness and unity underlying all things. Or as he put it at the end of *The Dry Salvages*, the last of the *Quartets*: "And the fire and the rose are one".

Meanwhile, Bruno Snell* - a very late Victorian: 1896-1986 - wrote *The Discovery of the Mind in Greek Philosophy and Literature* in Hamburg even as the RAF and USAAF bombed it into the ground. He advised Germans to follow the "Greek divinum rather than Greek humanum." He wanted his country to have what Pindar's Thebes had had - a world "effulgent with the divine" where the universal was discernible in the limited, and through which mankind could discern the eternal. Thebes was "spiritually rich and that to a poet is probably far more valuable than the quality we call genius or talent".

CHAPTER VII

Forgetting Obvious Things

There is something hard, repulsive, and ungrateful in the destructive instinct which so often forgets what has been done by the great men who proceeded us ... Those only should dare to utter the sacred name of Progress whose souls possess intelligence enough to comprehend the past, and whose hearts possess sufficient poetic religion to reverence its greatness. The temple of the true believer is not the chapel of a sect: it is a vast pantheon.

The industrial revolution has generated a new type of barbarism, with no roots in the past. For the second time in the history of Western Europe, continuity is in danger of being lost. A generation is growing up, not uneducated, but educated in a system which has little connexion with European culture in its historical development. The Classics are not taught; the Bible is not taught; history is not taught to any effect. What is even more serious, there are no social traditions. The modern townsman is déraciné: he has forgotten the habits and sentiments of the village from which his forefathers came.

DEAN INGE

G K Chesterton's *The Ballad of the White Horse* (1902) is about spiritual decay and renewal although the poem is centred on the story of King Alfred's last great battle in the West, against the Danes in May, 878. The Danes had over run all England except Wessex, Alfred's kingdom, and so the future of the English, and therefore of the world, revolved around that single day.

The Victorians, including Chesterton, thought the battle had been fought at Uffington in the Vale of the White Horse, the valley of the River Ock, a tributary of the Thames. The chalk hills on either side are the Berkshire Downs, nowhere quite reaching nine hundred feet. A Neolithic track called the Ridgeway runs from Dorset to Lincolnshire on the crest of the hills avoiding the wet and wooded Stone Age valleys. The Victorians also mistakenly thought that the White Horse, carved in the chalk of the hill, was a copy of the Saxon Royal Standard but it's most probably Bronze Age. The Horse in its entirety is visible only from the air so presumably it was meant to be seen by the gods alone. It's nearly four hundred feet long, carved in sinuous disconnected lines, an elongated outline of a galloping horse with one enormous eye in a head deftly suggested by a few simple strokes.

The battle, in fact, was fought at Ethandune, now Edington, in Wiltshire. Above the village is an escarpment, almost sheer, six or seven hundred feet high. The Danes under Guthrum held the high ground. They were professionals - if not professional soldiers then at least professional marauders. Given that, and given the terrain, the Danes should have won and in fact were winning until, late in the afternoon, thinking the battle was over, they slackened off. Alfred rallied his troops for a last assault on the hill which by now must have been slippery with blood.

After the battle, in the *Ballad* at least, Alfred ordered the scouring of the lines of the horse, cut in the turf, to uncover once more the whiteness of the chalk on the green hillside. A civilisation had been rescued and restored. Cleaning the chalk-white

horse symbolised renewal. The renewing of civilisation can never
stop:

> And if skies alter and empires melt,
> This word shall still be true:
> If we would have the horse of old,
> Scour ye the horse anew.

At the end of the *Ballad*, Alfred prophesies that the barbarians will be back. You'll know them by the ruins of their thought, the decay of intellect and reason, the denial of sin because, as Chesterton* also tells us, "Every high civilisation decays by forgetting obvious things".

PART FOUR

—

One Last Summer

Summary

How many minds really hand down the vast accumulations of the past? The number must be ludicrously small. A vigorous "dictatorship of the proletariat" might massacre the whole lot in six months. And each of them owns only one handful of the entire heap of erudition.

I will hazard the sweeping statement that the 19th was in many ways the most remarkable century since the beginning of history.

But my last word must be this. We cannot afford to throw away the wisdom of the past. It is too precious a treasure to be lost.

DEAN INGE

Inge was right: there *are* two realms, the material and the immaterial, eternity and time: lose one, lose both - the West has lost the higher and the lower is therefore on the blink. There are immaterial eternal values - Beauty, Goodness, the Truth. Regeneration has to come from inside, not through collectivist coercion. Religion, too, can only be understood from within - material evidence being neither possible nor needed: you have to make your own religion from your own inward experiences in accord with your own nature. Don't ask does God exist but rather what does the word God mean to you. You can't throw away nearly three thousand years of knowledge and cultural evolution and hope to invent something better from scratch: you need to know the past if you're to evolve something new and workable.

Ruskin also was right: the immaterial *is* more important than the material, and beauty and great art reunite us with it. Undertones of eternity can be daily reminders of this, along with sadness for the brevity and loneliness of things. Art mirrors the state of society but today both are broken and discordant. Ugliness - in art, ideologies, work or emotions, cities and land-scapes - is active and destructive and it dominates today. There is a law governing the way things have to be which we must obey to become complete as nature intended.

Arnold, Newman, Coleridge and Eliot were right: know-ing the best of what's been thought and said, the highlights of Western civilisation, do illuminate and set people free, let them see life steadily and see it whole. Without the spiritual you can't be free. Without the spiritual you can be sucked into a void of hatred and despair, rage, resentment, self-pity, spite and malevolence.

Eliot was right: you need a homogenous society with enough internal friction to generate ideas.

Coleridge was right: you need a clerisy.

Nietzsche was right: resentment is the default position of most of mankind.

Nietzsche and Hume were right: reason too often is pas-sion's slave, driven by resentment, damaged psychology or an ideology which is too narrow to see the whole, single stranded in a multi-stranded world.

Schopenhauer was right: we do mistake the limits of our vision for the limits of the world.

Noyes was almost right but, instead of hundreds of thou-sands of the elite chanting in unison a hymn of hate against all that is good, we now have millions, a stifling layer of the miseducated scorning and suffocating those beneath them.

Almost everything lies somewhere on a spectrum from good to bad and too many of the spiritually dispossessed know only the worst because they've never been taught the good, their teachers not knowing it themselves.

Vaughan Williams was right: great art is rooted in a place where people belong.

Huxley was right: without a meeting with the divine society degenerates into statism and revolution.

Alister Hardy was right: how can matter make non-matter? What is stranger than consciousness?

Gassendi was right: the immaterial is immortal.

Bishop Berkeley was right when he foretold the sly antics of Gramsci, Cultural Marxism, the French New Left and Post-Modernist Neo-Marxism: destroy the West by insinuating a new mindset into the elite, replacing the transcendent with a purely materialist creed.

Adorno/Horkheimer were right: Western culture and its art are tired and worn out, childish, smothered by a blanket of think-alikes.

Chesterton was right: the barbarians are back and we know them by the ruins of their thought, the decay of intellect and reason, the denial of sin.

Socrates was right: the unexamined life really is not worth living.

William James was right: the sense of eternity *is* a lyrical enchantment, a gift to life, and should be cherished.

Coleridge was right: without the spiritual which rides on culture who can be neither fully human nor free.

Arnold was right: culture is not about a having and getting but growing and becoming.

J A Stewart was right: Platonism is the love of the unseen and eternal cherished by one who rejoices in the unseen and temporal.

The soul senses eternity via the earth's beauty.

CHAPTER II

Last Word

By a hedge all overgrown
Hear the wartime bomber drone.

A heron with backward bending knees
Struts on the shoreline by the trees
As tide remakes a river:

Blue hills and headlands stretch away
From Plymouth Sound and Deadman's Bay.

The soul, they say, can still be free
On the gibbet or the gallows tree.

Lightning lit the spider's web
And thus was widow Dido wed.

A stoker in the hole
Is shovelling Cardiff coal
On a still red-dustered sea:

What do tides evoke?
Vernon in a grogham cloak:

Swap Manhattan for a nutmeg tree
After one great battle on the sea:

Sea-white rock of Quiberon
When the light has all but gone.

When did it go? That weight
Of summer on a loco
Softly breathing steam
By drooping willow and the stream?
On stone and lichen'd tile?
On pond and faded awning?
Summer smothering the vale
Which mankind broke, then mended?

Millennium came. I saw it go
In a fall of rain, a thaw of snow.

Defying nature always brings
Grief to an Icarus on brief wax wings:

Today the intellect is often bent
To thwart or hinder argument

For they've been taken in
By the folly of the Jacobin.

See the Godhead, like a saint,
In a splotch of yellow paint,
In sunlight on an ancient wall.

Where then is paradise?
Haloing Sadness, the imprecise.
Myopic shadows on a wall
Lift and flicker, blur, and fall

For I can show you the halo
Around the shade's shadow
If you in six o'clock sunshine
Can sense the divine.

Peace is therefore everywhere:
Rain stain on a brick,
Sunshine on a stair,

Carp arcing in a pond
Can let you see
Glimpses of eternity.

At last we know the rains do come
To your dry planet with its saffron sun.

Notes and Additions

William Ralph Inge (1860-1954), Dean of St Paul's, appears a lot in this book because he was one of the last of the Platonists, rare in itself but even rarer when you add acute insight and extreme readability. He came to Platonism in his early thirties and stuck by it for the next sixty years. Religion, he maintained, has to be based on an experience of the unseen. He believed this without, it seems, ever having had that experience himself. In *Outspoken Essays* (1921) he says: "I am very far from claiming that I have had these rich experiences myself ...The sweet sanctities of home life, and especially the innocence and affection of young children, more often bring me near to the felt presence of God."

Fox on Inge: "In aesthetic experience he must on the whole be judged deficient. Scenery delighted him more than art. Aesthetics was one of the few things perhaps about which he did not think much. Even in literature his strong sense of style was not aesthetic. Writing is for him a tool with which to express his thoughts. It is everywhere most lucid, and that could not be without craftsmanship but the craftsmanship nowhere obtrudes itself, not so much because the writer was artful enough to conceal his art, but because the thoughts he wished to express were themselves clear as crystal, and where the matter tended to grow difficult he stopped."

Fox adds that Inge "was a better judge of prose than of verse, partly because the best prose is that which tells the most, and in proportion as it does so it is the more acceptable to one who valued what he read for what it told him".

His father in later life was Provost of Worcester College, Oxford, although he'd still been a curate when his son was born, in Crayke in the Howardian Hills looking over the plain to York and its Minster. Inge went to Eton and then King's College, Cambridge. In an early photograph he looks not unlike G M Hopkins, also in an early photograph. For a time, Inge the Old Etonian taught young Etonians, not too successfully, it seems. For fifteen years from 1888 he was a Fellow and Tutor at Hertford College, Oxford, although he seems to have done little tutoring.

Depression and deafness marred his life - worsening deafness for all of it, depression until he married at the age of forty-five. He was ordained fairly late, aged thirty-two, probably because he needed to find a "sound intellectual basis" for belief, which he found in Platonism. Plotinus and Platonism were life long passions, and mysticism fascinated him to the end: he published his last book, *Mysticism in Religion*, when he was eighty-eight. For a couple of years at the beginning of the new century he was vicar of a fashionable church in Knightsbridge and then, briefly, Lady Margaret's Professor of Divinity in Cambridge. In 1911 he was invited to become Dean of St Paul's. He retired to Brightwell in Oxfordshire in 1934.

Almost every year for fifty years Inge published a new book, mostly lectures and collected newspaper articles: he wrote for *The Times, Daily Telegraph, Morning Post, Sunday Express, Manchester Guardian* - but also, and particularly, for the London *Evening Standard*: in the 1920s its editor paid him £20 a piece for his weekly column: that is roughly £900 in today's money, getting on for £45,000 a year, for one morning a week's work (as he claimed).

He had five children: a daughter died in 1923 from diabetes when she was twelve just as insulin was coming into use.

One son, a clergyman, was killed on a training flight with the RAF in 1941. Another son was an officer in the Somerset Light Infantry. The eldest boy seems to have been a civilian with the Anglo-Iranian Oil Company. His eldest daughter married a schoolmaster.

Adam Fox (1888-1977) was a Canon of Westminster from 1942 until 1959 when he was appointed Sub-Dean, retiring in 1963. In 1960, he published a life of Dean Inge, called *Dean Inge*. In it he explains the Platonism to which Inge adhered all his life.

J A Stewart (1846-1933) was a Professor of Philosophy in Oxford where he spent most of his life. (There are two John Alexander Stewarts: both Scots. The younger (1882-1948) was a colonial official in Burma: he was awarded the MC in the Great War and went on to compile the first Burmese-English dictionary.) J A Stewart gives this brief definition of Platonism in a lecture printed in *English Literature and the Classics* (1912).

Julian of Norwich (1342-c1416) was a Benedictine nun and anchoress who lived sealed in a cell in the church of St Julian in, of course, Norwich. We have an exact date for her mystical/Platonic experience: 8th May 1373. She left an account of what happened to her in *Showings* (or what she was shown to her). Oddly for a14th century nun, Julian believed that God and humanity are one and the same although the sense-soul doesn't know this because it's steeped in trivialities and the self. Sin isn't something you do. It's not a deed. It's the failure to be what we are meant to be, and an absence of love. We know it only by the pain it causes. Pain is a necessity: we need it for growth - without it there can be no bliss. T S Eliot quoted her most famous lines in *Little Gidding*:

> All shall be well and all shall be well, and
> All manner of thing shall be well.

Walter Terence Stace was the first, as far as I know, to use the words extrovertive and introvertive about mysticism. Paul's religion of the Spirit is introvertive: Plato's way of beauty is extrovertive. Stace was born a High Victorian in London in 1886 and died at Laguna Beach, California, eighty-one years later. From Fettes he went to Trinity, Dublin where he read philosophy. By then he seems to have had some kind of religious conversion and planned to become an Anglican priest. His family had other ideas and in 1910 the Colonial Office posted him to Ceylon, as Sri Lanka was then called. In his twenty years there he rose to be a magistrate or judge, I think, as well as mayor of Colombo. He thus missed the Great War. Instead, in the cool of each tropical morning, he wrote books on philosophy - well enough to get him asked, in 1932, to Princeton University. There, three years later, he was appointed Stuart Professor of Philosophy, and there he stayed until his retirement in 1955. Although an authority on Hegel, he was himself, unremarkably, an empiricist in the English-speaking tradition. More remarkably, in his mid-seventies he wrote two of the standard works on mysticism: *The Teachings of the Mystics* and *Mysticism and Philosophy* were published in the US in the same year, 1960.

He thought mysticism reveals something "supremely great in human life - "the peace which passeth all understanding". It's the gateway to salvation - "not in a future life but as the highest beatitude that a man can reach in this life, and out of which the greatest deeds of love can flow." Stace also said the mystic event is a"different kind of consciousness". It's different because it's void of all thought, feeling, emotion, ideas or concepts. It can't include any of these (at the highest level at least) because it's single, unbroken, with no room for anything but pure consciousness, conscious only of itself. It's complete and indivisible. Don't try thinking about it because reason can't reach it: you can experience it, that's all.

Stace begins *The Teachings of the Mystics* by saying what mysticism is not. It's not "misty, foggy, vague, or sloppy". Not "mystery-mongering". Not "the occult, spiritualism, ghosts or table turning". It's not about "telepathy, telekinesis, clairvoyance, precognition". (Inge had his own list: it isn't about "mysterious sights, sounds and smells, boisterous fits of weeping, cataleptic trances, stigmata, apparitions and the like".)

John Masefield (1878-1967) was the son of a solicitor in Ledbury, Herefordshire. When his mother died he lived with an aunt who sent him to the naval training ship *Conway* in the River Mersey to stop him from reading so much. In the 1890s he rounded the Horn in the barque *Gilcruix* on passage to Chile from where he was sent home by steamer suffering from sun stroke and a nervous breakdown. Judging by the sensitivity of his face in his portraits he was an unlikely seaman, particularly one sailing before the mast. His aunt thought otherwise; she sent him to join a Windjammer in New York (he was still a minor, aged only seventeen). He seems to have jumped ship before he even signed on and became a hobo, a barman, and then a carpet weaver. Back in England he married a woman a few years older than himself and they stayed together until she died, aged ninety, in 1960. In the Great War he served with the RAMC as an orderly both on the Western Front and then in charge of the ambulance boats at Gallipoli. Post-War he kept bees and goats on Boar's Hill in the Cumnor Hills across the river from Oxford. More importantly he had a private theatre in his garden for plays and poetry recitals. He also set up the Oxford Recitations to promote the art of verse speaking. On top of that he was Poet Laureate for thirty years - one of only three mystically inclined laureates (the others being Wordsworth and Tennyson).

Reginald Horace Blyth (1898-1964) was a conscientious objector in the Great War. Soon after it ended he married and went with his wife to the Far East: they lived in Korea for ten years in the 1920s and '30s. (They adopted a Korean boy. Years later, in 1947, the South Koreans shot him, thinking he was a traitor.) Blyth divorced his first wife and married a Japanese woman (they had two daughters). In 1940 they moved to Japan where he began teaching English literature at what later became Kanazawa University before being interned as an enemy alien when war broke out. Weirdly, he tried to take out Japanese citizenship in the middle of the War. If the Japanese had let him, he might have been hanged for treason. As it was he lived long enough to help draft the Mikado's denial of divinity and to teach English to the Crown Prince. Blyth, who was born in Essex (his father was a railway clerk), studied English in London University and left England for good in 1925. He seems to have read nothing in English later than that - including Eliot and Yeats, the last of the great English language poets.

Matthew Arnold divided the English into three classes - Barbarians, Philistines and the Populace. The Barbarians were the aristocracy, obsessed by manly exercises, sport, hunting, "vigour and good looks". These are external things: their minds were (although he thought the 18th century had been England's heyday - rule by noblemen and reason). The Populace was the lower working class, addicted to "marching were it likes, meeting where it likes, brawling where it likes, breaking what it likes". It also liked beer.

Arnold's main argument, however, was with the Philistines, the dissenting middle classes - shopkeepers, counting house clerks, chapel preachers - who lived in drab intellectual, aesthetic and spiritual poverty, trapped by self-deceiving smugness, obsessed with making money and cutting fine figures. They lacked, but needed, urbanity and delicacy: they were far too parochial and had to become cosmopolitan. By their narrowness and aloofness from their own civilisation they diminished themselves and everybody else. They also needed the grace and fantasy of their own Celtic fringe. Industrialism was not the cause - their mind-set dated back to 17th century Puritanism. Arnold knew them personally through his work as a school inspector.

The English were good practical reasoners and thinkers (Britain was still the world's workshop) but weak on the purer kind. Hellenism is about "the desire to get rid of one's ignorance, to see things as they are, and by seeing them as they are to see them in their beauty".

By **Hebraism** Arnold meant a thoroughly de-Hellenised Christianity cut back to what he thought was 1st century Judaism. Jesus personalised, emotionalised and revealed the basic rules of life. The essence of good conduct and living is self-sacrifice, of abandoning the self. Look within and you'll find your best self and so find your soul, which it is. "For the power of Christianity has been in the immense emotion which it has excited: in its engaging, for the government of man's conduct, the mighty forces of love, reverence, gratitude, hope, pity, awe." The Cross is the ultimate symbol of self-sacrifice, of living for others, the final assault on the ego. The Bible, he believed, has to be read as literature, as poetry, with all the depth that reading adds to the human soul.

Arnold's father had a cottage near the Wordsworths in Ambleside and so Matthew, as a boy, knew the poet personally. He mistook Wordsworth's mysticism, inspired by the Cumbrian fells, for his own milder pleasure in the Cumnor Hills. However he did seem to know that thought blocks something, but not what was blocked. Being unable to let go of self-consciousness was, he also knew, the problem. He experienced a sense of greaterness but linked it to uprightness, honesty and common decency. What some call God can be glimpsed on the edge of consciousness. Beauty, he also realised, makes us bigger and better and poetry almost certainly gave him some kind of religious experience. Then, in 1879 in an essay on Byron, he finally recognised the value of Wordsworth's joy in nature as being "healthful and true." It was also moral because it shows us how to live.

Arnold's father - Thomas - was headmaster of Rugby School, turning out muscular Christians (as in *Tom Brown's Schooldays* (1857)). Matthew Arnold went first to Winchester College and then, in the 5th and 6th Forms, Rugby. At Balliol College, Oxford, he teamed up with Arthur Henry Clough (1819-1861), the Thyrsis of the memorial poem. Arnold died in 1888 of a heart attack brought on by rushing to catch a train in Liverpool where his daughter was disembarking after a trip to America. By then he'd lost three of his five children.

Eleusinian Mysteries: in the 5th century BC, thousands of people massed, after two days without food, on a beach near Athens before marching to Eleusis, calling on Dionysus, the god of change, as they went. They reached the town at sunset and began wandering by torchlight, lost and disorientated, through the streets before being herded into the blackness of a great unlit hall. There they watched, presumably in some kind of spot light, an animal sacrifice, followed by something "unspeakable", perhaps the acted-out killing of a child. A play of some sort re-enacted Demeter's reunion with her daughter, Persephone, back from Hades, a kind of resurrection. In a slightly different version, people washed themselves spiritually clean in two salt-water lakes as well as in the sea. The sacramental food in the big shed was barley-meal, honey and water. An ear of corn (standing for Demeter) was revealed, perhaps held high like the wafer in the eucharist. By then receptive minds would have shut down, all thought stopped, and they'd have experienced eternity or the beatific vision.

Evidence from Antiquity suggests the Mysteries really worked. Diodorus (fl.1st century BC) says, referring to the Samothracian Mysteries, that "those who have taken part in them are said to become more pious, more upright, and in every way better than their former selves." If it worked then, presumably it worked for some in the Roman and Greek churches all down the ages. (Orthodox monks still practise a form of meditation called *hesychasm* (stillness, peace or silence) inherited from their Platonist forebears: sit quietly, chin on chest, look inward, control breath, intone (mantra-like) the Jesus Prayer: "Lord Jesus Christ, Son of God, have mercy on me, a sinner".)

Protestants are not less **mystical** than everybody else: William James's *The Varieties of Religious Experience*, for example, is largely based on studies of Evangelicals. All mystics, he writes, believe "that the visible world is part of a more spiritual universe from which it draws its chief significance … that union or harmonious relation with that higher universe is our true end". Religion confers "a new zest which adds itself like a gift to life, and takes the form … of lyrical enchantment". At the core of all religion, James argues, is "an individual's experience of what he regards as the divine … Without the divine, all are potentially sick". The problem is that Protestantism's tendency to a stripped down, verbal, ritual-limited, literal Bible Christianity can too easily exclude a sense of the numinous.

Caroline Spurgeon was born in India in 1869. Her mother died giving birth to her, while her father - an officer in the Herefordshire Regiment - died only five years later. She was educated at Cheltenham Ladies' College and London University from where she went on to an academic career, eventually becoming Professor of English in Bedford College, London, in 1913 - he first female professor in London, the second in England. That same year she published *Mysticism and English Literature*, an original work since, as far as I know, nobody before her had realised how many English writers were mystics. Her book is very short - under forty thousand words - and Plato is mentioned by name over fifty times. She asked: "what does the mystic see?" and replied: "Unity underlying diversity." "Mystics," she says, "are the only people in the world who are possessors of certainty. They have seen, they have felt; what need they of further proof? Logic, philosophy, theology are empty sounds and barren forms to those who know."

In 1918 she went to the United States with the British Educational Mission. There she met Virginia Gildersleeve, an academic at Columbia University, who was later involved in writing the UN Charter. After that, they spent every summer together until Spurgeon's death in 1942 in Tucson, Arizona, where she'd gone in 1936 because the climate eased the pain of her arthritis. She's also known for a study of Shakespeare's imagery and *Five Hundred Years of Chaucer Criticism and Allusion, 1357–1900* (1929). She was not herself a mystic or even a Platonist in spite of her insights.

Romain Rolland (1866-1944) tells us in *Journey Within* (1947) about his first mystical experience at the age of fifteen. In the summer of 1882 he visited Voltaire's house in Ferney. As he stepped outside he experienced a sense of "unity". Later, in 1885/6, reading Spinoza made him realise that everything, himself included, was part of God. He experienced that unity as peace.

Rolland was a French novelist, playwright, art historian, musicologist, Nobel Laureate, pacifist, vegetarian and, of course, a mystic - but not a Platonist: instead he turned east to Vedanta. Very oddly he was also a Stalinist (in 1996 Russia commemorated Rolland's life with a four kopek postage stamp). Rolland was the first, I understand, to use "oceanic" in a spiritual sense.

Helen Darbishire (1881–1961) was the Principal of Somerville College, Oxford, 1931-1945. She retired to the Lake District where she was a trustee of Dove Cottage.

Coleridge believed that Western mankind divides into Platonists (who favour the disembodied mind or soul) and Aristotelians (who favour body *and* soul). St Augustine was a Platonist, St Thomas Aquinas was an Aristotelian as was **Francis Bacon** (Lord Verulam, 1561-1626). The Ancients were young, he argued, and therefore his own generation was old and so in need of a new beginning. Don't we awed by those youngsters, the Greeks of Antiquity, he advised: take a new route - technical schools, not the Oxbridge colleges, study geography and the effects of climate on the locals, follow the concrete rather than the abstract. We can't learn new things through arguing about old abstractions and we don't want to be spiders weaving webs from our own minds, or like ants collecting data: we need to be bee-like, gathering knowledge and turning what we've learned into something materially useful. He was, he said of himself, like an orchestra tuning up - discordant noise but soon to be followed by music. His was an untried method, he admitted, but worth trying and of course we in the West did and prospered.

Bacon's *New Organon* (1620) was a reply to the old one in which Aristotle first systematised logic. Organon means tool. Logic was Aristotle's tool for aiding thought, inductive reasoning was Bacon's. Bacon's book, in fact, is the foundational document of modern science. Inductive reasoning or reductionism means gathering a mass of particulars and then working out a general theory to explain them. But we had to wait for Karl Popper (1902-1994) to complete the scientific method: you can never prove a theory is right but you can falsify it, or prove it's wrong. "All swans are white" is the example he gives in *The Open Society* (1945). For thousands of years Europeans only ever saw white swans and therefore concluded that all swans are white. Then a ship sailed into the Swan River in Western Australia where all the swans were black.

Popper blamed Plato for the 20th century's statist dictatorships, particularly the ideas in *The Republic*, though he was seemingly unaware of the old man's mystical side. Francis Bacon was only twelve when he went to Cambridge. In Queen Elizabeth's reign, he was a Member of Parliament for several places from Dorset to Liverpool. He argued for a United Kingdom before the union of the Crowns. Later he prospered under King James: knighthood, Attorney General, Lord Chancellor, created Viscount St Alban, until he was accused of bribery and retired to study and write. He died of pneumonia after experimenting with refrigeration - stuffing a dead chicken with snow in Pond Square, Highgate, when there really was a pond there.

Harold Bloom (1930-2019) was a Professor of English at Yale who taught his last class four days before he died, aged eighty-nine. *The Western Canon* (1994) is both an overview of our greatest literature but also a defence of the Canon itself against what he called the "School of Resentment" - a school made up of those proliferating and splintering groups on the left who've set out to destroy the West itself by destroying Arnoldian culture. "The idea that you benefit the insulted and injured by reading someone of their own origins rather than reading Shakespeare is one of the oddest illusions ever promoted by or in our schools". Self-knowledge and taking pleasure in beauty, he thought, were the main reasons for keeping and reading the Canon. He seems to have been interested in Gnosticism, not Platonism.

Bloom on Shakespeare: On the other hand, Chaucer's Wife of Bath is no cardboard cutout and Sir Philip Sidney began *Astrophel and Stella* with "... look in thy heart and write". Montaigne invented the essay just to study his own mind: "What do I know?" John Florio, who translated Montaigne, knew Shakespeare personally. Know Thyself was chiselled on the lintel of the Temple at Delphi and Socrates told us the unexamined life is not worth living.

Jacques Barzun (1907-2012) was ninety-two when he published his last book, *From Dawn to Decadence,* as the old century came to its weary end. Its theme is the final decline of the West. It's a chronicle of the breaking down of boundaries, oppressive or irksome, but also boundaries dictated by the nature of things. A lesser theme is the need to belong. At the same time, increasing complexity sends people in search of simplicity, a past simplicity or a made up one. In a way, it's about the breaking down of society which Ibsen's absence of insight initiated over a hundred years earlier.

Emancipation has now reached its logical conclusion in a deadlock of conflicting freed egos with no general, culture-wide, over-all sense of purpose, no more possibilities, only comfort-seeking in mini-cults like climate change, environmentalism, socialism. Millions of the lost are milling about - denying, debunking, lashing out, searching for simplicity in complexity. Nobody belongs to the whole: there is only fragmentation, gridlock, log jam, stalemate, overwhelming diversity: people are for/against collectivism/individualism, high art/low art, irreligion/religion. Rights are bandied around and handed out indiscriminately to "illegal immigrants, children, criminals, babies, plants, animals." There is a longing for the primitive and the simple. At the same time, old art forms are worked out and institutions can no longer evolve. This civilisation is stale with nothing to offer but repetition, boredom, fatigue and an unhappy search for the spiritual. This is a "stalled society", filled with vitality and energy but deadlocked. New ideas are instantly opposed by contrarian groups, and all this amid a "floating hostility to things as they are". By getting rid of the old, people think, a new good will spontaneously arise. The new will fill the void, the vacuum, the pit. Failing that, take your resentment out on helpless others. Reason has given way to the unreasonable, the rational to malign irrationality.

Poetry of Ideas: In the 8th century BC, Hesiod, a farmer in Boeotia, expressed his simple philosophy of success-through-work in a poem. In the 5th and 6th centuries Parmenides (nothing changes) and Empedocles (everything changes) wrote their treatises in verse. Xenophanes was a poet who turned to philosophy for ideas to versify. Virgil's Georgics tells us how to raise horses and keep bees. In the 1st century BC Lucretius versified Epicureanism. Ovid shows us how to avoid getting hurt by love. Dante's Divine Comedy is about Aquinan or Aristotelian Christianity. Milton's Paradise Lost fits the didactic genre, along with Pope's Essays on Man and Criticism. (The heroic, said Barzun, is "the philosophic couplet par excellence".) Shelley's

Queen Mab is about Godwinism although the poet was also a Platonist and proto-socialist. Tennyson's In Memoriam asks is there an afterlife? and finds no answer except choose to believe. BV's The City of Dreadful Night is about the agony of spiritual emptiness, a void filled only by pain. Kipling's If offers words to live by. Eliot's The Wasteland and Four Quartets are about the ruins of a civilisation caused by the loss of the spiritual and the search for renewal through the transcendent. Robert Bridges versified Platonism in *A Testament of Beauty*. He failed, I think, because the way he said it lacks both beauty and clarity.

Empedocles on Etna: The curious thing about Matthew Arnold is that he skirted round and round mysticism, knew its causes and its effects, but never quite got there. He sensed that thought is the problem, and non-thought the answer, but was never able to stop himself from thinking. You can see how close he got to the answer in *Empedocles on Etna* which he wrote in 1849 when he was only twenty-seven. *Empedocles* is a short narrative poem; short on narrative, long on argument. Empedocles himself is the pre-Socratic materialist philosopher who was born in 490 BC and whose evolution theory predates Darwin's by the best part of two and half thousand years though his ideas are distinctly peculiar: animals evolved with - say - one leg and two heads and other oddities until nature itself weeded out the most improbable and (therefore) impractical. More famously he said that everything is made of earth, air, fire, and water and that the powers of Love and Strife (Eros and Eris) control and mix them (people quarrel and fall in love, if you need proof). (But see below this note for the originator of these ideas.)

In the poem Empedocles is (or was: he's lost his power) a miracle-worker who could calm the storm and cure old age. Pausanias, his companion, was also an historical figure. In real life he'd been Empedocles's catamite, as was the custom in Antiquity. Callicles, the harpist and bard, is invented although his songs are based on Pindar and Ovid.

The story is simple. The Greek colonies in Italy are unsettled by Sophistry, the philosophy which says anything goes - half lies, lies, deceit, statistics - as long as you win, which is defined as closing down the argument: there's no such thing as truth, only a victor and a silenced opponent. Empedocles can take this corruption no more and sets off to kill himself in the volcano. (In reality he didn't die on Etna, although an under-sea volcano off the coast of Sicily is named after him.) Pausanias goes with him part of the way - for his own ends as much as anything else. Callicles is part of the plot for one reason only - to illustrate a better way of looking at things. His ideas border on the minor mystical, but don't cross over because Arnold himself never got beyond that frontier.

A sub-theme of wet and dry, arid and fertile, sunshine and shade runs through the whole poem. Callicles stays hidden in woods by the streams on the lower slopes. Empedocles climbs across the cindery-dry pumice through harsh sunlight to the top of the cone of the volcano.

Four philosophies are broached. Pausanias is an extravert and an externalist - everything that happens to people is caused by events outside themselves. (Both Callicles and Empedocles disagree: the answer is almost always within.) Pausanias thinks that Empedocles had once been able to raise the dead. If he could find out how, he too could defy the gods and live free of fear forever.

Empedocles has two things to say to him, and the first is meant as wages to pay Pausanias for his services and to help him live without his master's company. People's problems are caused by limited understanding and vision, he begins: souls are like mirrors swinging on strings in the wind: they see in part and in snatches. But because we can see only piecemeal doesn't mean there isn't a meaningful whole. People invented gods, he goes on un-Platonically, because they need something to blame for the mess they make of their lives. The need for happiness is wired in, but nobody has a right to it. Unhappiness is caused by the mismatch of what people want and what they have. Youth wants rapture and chases it. But life is short and, when they don't find it, they look to an afterlife to give it to them. People waste their lives waiting for death. Everything - gods, cosmos, people - is made of the same material so how can you hate what you're made of? Is living with love and sunlight so small a thing that you long for death? All you can do is make the most of what you have, and don't despair.

But Empedocles no longer lives by this philosophy. When he's alone on the rim of the crater, we learn what he truly thinks. Philosophy and thought are a hindrance and get in the way of truth. Mind and thought are wrong for this world. Thinkers are aliens because thought blocks access to the Under-Reality, the All.

But for Empedocles there's another snag: he's a Stoic rein-carnationist who believes the same troubles will follow him through life after life in an everlasting loop of time: all he can do is stop the pain in each of those appalling lives by repeatedly killing himself. He leaps into Etna's boiling crater, as he will do forever - yet in those few moments of free-fall, thought stops and (we assume) he's in touch with eternity. We assume because Arnold doesn't say, and Arnold didn't say because he didn't know.

Meanwhile, Callicles feels the volcano heave and shake: he watches the flames flare as Empedocles burns. Immediately afterwards he sees Apollo and the Nine Muses ("their garments out-glistening/The gold-flower'd broom") stop to swim in a pool before going on to their home on Olympus. They glorify the Creator, they glorify the nature of things, glorify the peace of the immortals, they glorify ...

The day in his hotness,
The strife in the palm;
The night in her silence,
The stars in their calm.

Apollo, of course, is the god of clarity and light, music and the intellect. Callicles, the bard, instinctively knows the secret which eludes the thinking man: salvation comes through art and "the daily miracle of common things".

(Anaximander (c610-c546 BC) was, in fact, the first **evolutionist:** life began in mud created by the tensions between opposing forces - hot/cold, wet/dry - working on a limitless chaos of matter, otherwise known as the everlasting Boundless. At first there were only scaly fishes but eventually scale-free people evolved. He also argued that the earth is shaped like a barrel held in space by the same opposing energies: we live on the flat upended top bit.)

Samuel Palmer had only two terms of formal schooling (at Merchant Taylors'). On the other hand his father was a bookseller and the boy read a lot. On top of that, he had a private drawing master and went to Flaxman's lectures in the Royal Academy: when he was seventeen he'd already sold one picture and exhibited three others, all under Turner's influence, in the RA's summer hangings. John Linnell (1792-1882) noticed him and pointed the boy artistically backwards. "Heaven sent him," Palmer later said, "to pluck me from the pit of modern art." Linnell, who later became his father-in-law, also introduced him to Blake,

Palmer was born just off the Old Kent Road and, judging by a self-portrait painted when he was about twenty, his face was that of typical south London Cockney, except for the sadness in the eyes. As a boy he had no friends of the same age, played no outdoor games and only backgammon indoors. His father, the book seller, was also a lay Baptist preacher: the rest of the family were well-heeled felt-makers in the City. Mary Ward, his nurse, saved him from vitamin deficiency at the hands of his unskilled mother - who died when he was thirteen: he said the pain of it was like being pierced with a sword. Mary also dressed him oddly even when he was a man in his twenties: she sewed pockets on his coat big enough for two painter's palettes and books. Small boys mocked him because his hats were too big and his legs too short for his normally sized body. On her death bed Mary gave him a copy of Milton's shorter poems which he reinforced with brass and carried for twenty years in his waistcoat pocket. (Mary also turned up in the Valley of Vision, along with Palmer's father who'd been bribed by his felt-making brother to give up book selling in order to live like a gentleman.)

Palmer married Linnell's daughter, Hannah, in 1837. Linnell went on to make a fortune, while the Palmers often relied on him for help. In London most of Palmer's earned income was from teaching and he was nearly fifty before he became a full member of the Watercolour Society and so could hang his work in public.

He lost his sense of eternity - "those delicious visions which are the only joys of my life" - around the time he married and - in consequence? - his happiness and talent.

Ralph Vaughan Williams was born in Gloucestershire but in 1872, when he was three, his mother took him to Leith Hill Place, her old home. Leith Hill, just short of a thousand feet, is the highest point in Surrey. Their house is on the lower slopes but high enough to see across the Low Weald to the South Downs. The Low Weald is so well wooded it looks like a forest and the Downs are distant enough to be blue. King Alfred the Great's father, Ethelwulf, defeated the Danes here in 851. A mass grave, possibly of men who fought there, was unearthed when young Ralph was ten.

For a mystically inclined child Leith Hill must have been more like a portal than a place, opening onto that ultimate reality he spoke about. Childhood should have been perfect - kindness and culture, money and space (the walled kitchen garden across the lane from the big house is four acres on its own). The family woods had been inter-planted with azaleas and rhododendrons. Old stone pits had returned to nature as ponds, some big enough for swimming in. When he was older he had an organ in the hall where he practised before breakfast. Working the bellows was the problem: the butler had to lay the table, a groom or gardener was corralled occasionally. More usually it was one of the maids who was then put behind with her work. Not a lot of science was taught but at least Great-Uncle Charles, who tipped half a crown when he visited, was the author of *The Origins of Species*. (As girls, Vaughan Williams's mother and aunt were asked to do research for him. Are the stalks of the bird's nest orchis straight or curved when they first sprout?) The night he died, in his sleep, he was still working, planning a future.

Ruskin stumbled on the **Law of Help** in his early twenties while sketching ivy and thorns in Norwood and then an aspen in Fontainebleau. Two years later, now aged twenty-six, he was in the Cathedral in Lucca in Tuscany when he came across Jacopo della Quercia's carving of Ilaria del Carretto, a young woman (also aged twenty-six) who died in 1405. Ruskin recognised that the "harmonies of line" in the statue "were under the same laws as the river wave, and the aspen branch, and the stars' rising and setting". In other words, great art also obeys the laws which order and structure physical things. In Lucca's Medieval buildings, too, he detected the same eternal blueprint which ensured their greatness.

In a letter home, **A E Housman** records one of Ruskin's lectures in Oxford in the late 1870s or early '80s. (Ruskin was Slade Professor of Fine Art): "This afternoon Ruskin gave us a great outburst against modern times. He had got a picture of Turner's, framed and glassed, representing Leicester and the Abbey in the distance at sunset, over a river. He read the account of Wolsey's death out of Henry VIII. Then he pointed to the picture as representing Leicester when Turner had drawn it. Then he said, "You, if you like, may go to Leicester to see what it is like now. I never shall. But I can make a pretty good guess." Then he caught up a paintbrush. "These stepping-stones of course have been done away with, and are replaced by a be-au-tiful iron bridge."

Then he dashed in the iron bridge on the glass of the picture. "The colour of the stream is supplied on one side by the indigo factory." Forthwith one side of the stream became indigo. "On the other side by the soap factory." Soap dashed in. "They mix in the middle - like curds," he said, working them together with a sort of malicious deliberation. "This field, over which you see the sun setting behind the abbey, is not occupied in a proper manner." Then there went a flame of scarlet across the picture, which developed itself into windows and roofs and red brick, and rushed up into a chimney. "The atmosphere is supplied - thus!" A puff and cloud of smoke all over Turner's sky: and then the brush thrown down, and Ruskin confronting modern civilisation amidst a tempest of applause, which he always elicits now, as he has this term become immensely popular, his lectures being crowded, whereas of old he used to prophesy to empty benches."

Ralph Vaughan Williams (1872-1958), composer, conductor, atheist and mystic, also thought all great art is rooted in a sense of **belonging** to a country with a continuity of history, art, law, philosophy, customs and shared memories (folk music was the embodiment of a country's deepest being). More than that, without these things there can be no art at all. "A colourless cosmopolitanism may produce a crowd of dilettante gourmets, but it will never produce a creative artist." Art can be global only if it's local to begin with: you can't create a garden where wild flowers won't grow. This wasn't jingoism, he insisted. Still less was it nationalism, or even patriotism: it was a fact of life.

In the early 20th century Vaughan Williams gave a series of lectures on folk music. Astonishingly, in a country where folk songs were still sung without affectation in village ale houses, he got his lecture notes from a book. Worse, the material had been collected sixty years earlier by a man who had also lived, by a strange twist of coincidence, on Leith Hill, the composer's boyhood home. In 1903 Vaughan Williams lectured in Essex. Two ladies in his audience asked him if he'd like to meet a real folk singer in their own village of Ingrave. Through them he met an old shepherd called Charles Pottipher who sang *Bushes and Briars* for him. After that, he began collecting for himself. He also began using folk music in his own work. *In the Fen Country* dates from this time (1904), a *Norfolk Rhapsody* from two year later. Both are based on folk songs he'd collected - in particular from King's Lynn where the Viking-descended fishermen still lived apart from the rest of the town.

The Victorians of course had no idea what **socialism** and communism would be like. Wilde, for example, wrote *The Soul of Man Under Socialism* a quarter of a century before Lenin's Red Revolution. To begin with, Wilde's socialism was not about the collective or the statist but about setting the individual free. Property ownership is a bore because it entails tiresome duties. Socialism would abolish property and, with it, poverty. Socialism is about being, not owning or having. Without property all can live, not just exist. You can create the perfect man if you have perfect conditions. Under socialism, true personality will flourish and grow naturally without argument or discord. People will know everything, own nothing: it will be beautiful, with no jealousy, no laws, no authority. There'll be no punishments at all because punishment increases crime: what little crime there might be will be treated by doctors as the mental illness it is. Criminals aren't criminals at all - they're people who are starving. It won't be a question of know thyself but be thyself. "Develop your perfection within. Riches are within. Material things not only don't matter, they get in the way of inner growth." Socialism will also abolish marriage and the family, which was what Jesus wanted. You can't conform and be free. The state will make what is useful: individuals will make what is beautiful. All disgusting manual work will be done by machines - coal mining, stoking furnaces, running messages. Until now, machines have put men out of work to enrich a single owner: under Socialism all will benefit. Under socialism, Wilde ends, there'll be no diseases, no dull work, only "joy in the contemplation of the joyous life of others."

Fors Clavigera: The title means, roughly, now is the right time to hit the nail on the head and change things. Fors- (Force), -gera (bearer or carrier) and clava, clavis, clavus - club (of Hercules), key (of Ulysses), nail. There might also be a bit of punning on the English syllable for-: force, fortitude, fortune. Ruskin got the idea from an ode by Horace

Architects: How can you arrive at Brutalist buildings if you follow Ruskin's advice? "Among the first habits that a young architect should learn is that of thinking in shadow, not looking at a design in its miserable liny skeleton; but conceiving it as it will be when the dawn lights it and the dusk leaves it; when the stones will be hot, and its crannies cool; the lizards will bask on the one, and the birds build on the other. Let him design with the sense of cold and heat upon him; let him cut out the shadows, as men dig wells in unwatered plains; and lead along the lights, as a founder does his hot metal; let him keep full command of both, and see that he knows how they fall, and where they fade."

In the summer of 1803 - a few weeks after the birth of his first child (whose mother was none too pleased) - Wordsworth set off out on a six week tour of Scotland with **Dorothy** and Coleridge in an Irish jaunting car. (Coleridge gave up half way, the Wordsworths pressed on.) Gilpin, the apostle of the picturesque had been there before them - in 1776, when they were all still children. 1790 to 1810 was the height of the picturesque craze. Dorothy denied they were prospect-hunters or "picturesque travellers". Wordsworth and Coleridge, in fact, rejected picturesqueness - it came at nature from the wrong angle, from a false premise (nature can't copy art) and so was incapable of seeing the countryside in all its reality, an impoverished peasantry included. For Wordsworth, also, the Sublime came in two parts - it could both terrify *and* close down thought to induce a sense of eternity. Coleridge seems to have thought of the sublime as boundless infinity (hence the importance of the ocean in the *Mariner*).

So what were they after? The whole 1803 Tour of Scotland was about finding, relishing and later remembering beauty spots of a kind they couldn't find in England. Wordsworth also got a few poems out of it, two at least of great value. (They came across the Gaelic-singing *Solitary Reaper*, for example, near Loch Voil on their way back over the Trossachs:

Perhaps the plaintive numbers flow
For old unhappy far-off things,
And battles long ago.)

They met Walter Scott in a street in Melrose where he was on business as the Sheriff of Selkirk. He showed them over the ruined abbey, pointing out sculptures they wouldn't otherwise have noticed. Dorothy loved the place and its early Gothic shapes but said the prospect was spoiled by "insignificant houses" which hemmed it in. It was also too far from the river in a "broken and disturbed" vale. Worse was the ultimate dismal barbarism of putting "the ugliest church you ever beheld" inside its romantically ruined shell. The church floor was also unpaved and the damp made it dangerous to sit there. The bare, bleak uplands of Lowland Scotland also distressed her and she didn't much like fir trees, either: pine plantations were "forever at war with simplicity".

In the Highlands, they took Mr Gilpin's Short Tour (they had his guide book), missing out Loch Ness, a straight and narrow bit of water which wouldn't have been right for them either. In fact in the whole of Scotland, a depopulated land, she found only one or two places which had what they were looking for or which at least excited her. The first was the scatter of islands - large, small, flat, hilly, wooded, one with an arched ruin - seen from the top of Inchtavannach, the Isle of Monks, in Loch Lomond. Islands were important to her: the Wordsworths kept a boat for fishing but also for picnics on the island in their own Grasmere.

But Loch Katrine in the Trossachs was their Shangri-La. They walked to it over the mountains from Loch Lomond and Dorothy was instantly transported - by the bays ("bays within bays"), by the lake's solitary island, by Ben Venue, pleasingly un-smooth with craggy outcrops and no single summit, draped with birches. "The place was all eye, and completely satisfied the sense and the heart ... The feeling of excessive beautifulness overcomes every other". Loch Achray over the mountains in the next glen was made for the "comforts of man", Katrine for "the lonely delight of nature, and kind spirits delighting in beauty". It was so right they changed their plans, left the horse and jaunting car in Callander, and walked back over the mountains to revisit. The loch was now in sunshine, unlike the mistiness of their first visit. This time they were rowed "under steep crags hung with birches." She tells us how she felt as they rowed away from the sunset on bright water under untouched hills: "It was like a new-discovered country of which we had never dreamed..."

Young adulthood was her period though she had Wordsworth to herself for only seven years. She then more or less settled down as the eternal maiden aunt, the useful spinster good for nursing the sick or helping with the very young or very old. She was housekeeping for John, Wordsworth's oldest son (a curate in Leicestershire), when she was taken seriously ill with gall bladder problems, a sickness from which she never really recovered.

She lost her mind around the age of sixty but lived for another twenty-three years, hugging the summertime fire, fretful sometimes, sometimes violent and shrill, screaming, "making blowing noises", refusing to be taken out in her wheelchair, at times delighted by the cuckoo in the cuckoo clock, a gift of Isabella Fenwick (because Wordsworth loved cuckoos) on the upstairs landing, reciting her brother's poetry by the ream. Arteriosclerosis (thickening and hardening of the arteries), cholecystitis (inflammation of the gallbladder) or gallstones were once suggested as the cause. Thiamin or vitamin B1 deficiency is a more recent explanation. Her journals were published in 1897.

In the Spring of 1838, she wrote a final letter, strangely suffused with undertones of eternity, to her niece Dora: "Poor Peggy Benson lies in Grasmere Church-yard beside her once beautiful mother. Fanny Haigh is gone to a better world. My Friend mrs Rawson has ended her ninety and two years pilgrimage - and *I* have fought and fretted and striven - and am here beside the fire. The Doves behind me at the small window - the laburnum with its naked seed-pods shivers before my window and the pine-trees rock their base".

In some ways **Coleridge** was a prototype 21st century Westerner - a drug addict with a broken marriage, a failure in love, a left-winger who belonged to the very first left wing generation of them all. In later in life, he moved to the right as so many are still said to do. In the end he was a kind of Tory with a social consciousness - give the poor a stake in society for stability's stake, and tame capitalism.

The highlights - or lows - of his life are often quoted. He tried to kill his brother with a knife over a bit of toasted cheese when they were boys in Ottery St Mary, their father's parish in Devon. As a Blue Coat Boy at Christ's Hospital he swam or waded fully clothed in the New River (a canalised aqueduct) in north London and fell ill with jaundice and rheumatic fever (he's still of interest to medical historians because he was a life-long note-keeping hypochondriac given to quack remedies). He ran away from Cambridge to join the 15th Light Dragoons though he couldn't sit a horse. Jesus College took him back after his brothers got him out of the Army, pleading insanity. He left Cambridge without a degree. Already he was writing - sonnets for the London papers, to begin with. After that he never stopped writing or lecturing or talking for the rest of his life: letters, reviews, articles, complete magazines, poetry, lectures, and books.

With Southey, in their young days, he planned a Utopia in Pennsylvania to make people perfect by removing temptation. It came to nothing but he'd already married, unhappily, Southey's sister-in-law before it failed. Friends were already helping him: he had an annuity from the Wedgwood brothers until the war ruined them. Tom Poole let him have the house next to his tannery in Nether Stowey. Cottle, the Bristol publisher, introduced him to the Wordsworths (and published *Lyrical Ballads*).

After nearly a year in Germany, where he'd gone to study Idealism, he took his wife and family to live on the shores of Derwentwater to be near the Wordsworths. He fell in love with Wordsworth's sister-in-law, Sara Hutchinson. It was unreturned. He took time off to sail to Malta in a wartime military convoy to find himself. He didn't. Back in the Lakes he wrote, edited, and paid for another failed magazine, *The Friend,* with Sara's help. That was before the final split with the Wordsworths (they called him "a rotten drunkard" behind his back). A spiral down into drugged and drunken despair ended in a suicidal nervous breakdown, in Bath of all genteel places (he was lecturing there) after which Dr Gillman took him home to Highgate.

His house in The Grove is still there (J B Priestley occupied it for a time) just across the road from The Flask, a 17th century inn which was being rebuilt in Coleridge's early days in the area. The inn, a place of dozens of tiny rooms, is said to be haunted: Dick Turpin, it's also said, hid in the wine cellar and Hogarth certainly drank there (beer, presumably, not gin). Pond Square, where Bacon tried to refrigerate a chicken, is nearby. Kenwood House, along the crest of hills, was still the original 17th century mansion in Coleridge's time (rebuilding began thirty years after his death). In its grounds you can still get a flavour of those hills of groves and villas which Carlyle wrote about: it's above a deep valley, with several small streams or rills and artificial lakes (one's called The Thousand Pound Pond - the cost of excavating and damming it, I believe). The hills are sand on clay: ponds, wells, and small rills are everywhere along the spring line (the inn-keeper sold flasks to people who wanted to take the water home - hence the inn's name). Coleridge's opium habit eased off but he never broke it entirely. He died of a heart attack in the summer of 1834.

At one time, Wordsworth thought **most people are mystically inclined** but, like illiterates, they can't read what's written in the nature of things. R S Thomas was one such. He was, by all accounts, a strange old man, bitter and hate-ridden, but also a professional Christian, an Anglican priest, who spent his life searching for the God whose word he preached. He edited a book of Wordsworth's verse, and wrote the Introduction, without ever once realising that he was reading about the God he looked for. And also, as Wordsworth's own cased proved, the literate can forget how to read and are diminished by it.

Wordsworth himself may have had one last late experience, when he was thirty-eight, not on the fells in summer but in winter in London at the foot of Ludgate Hill looking up at St Paul's through lightly falling snow. Fleet Street was "silent, empty, and pure white, with a sprinkling of new fallen snow, not a cart or carriage to obstruct the view: no noise, only a few soundless and dusky foot passengers here and there" - the classic setting of sadness and stillness.

Schelling, in one of several of his philosophies, thought that **Nature** is forever evolving through stones, plants and people. Nature is a oneness and a process. It's creative and so the artist is the highest kind of evolved matter, an idea welcome to Romantic poets. This philosophy is teleological - creative art is the end which drove Nature onwards from the very beginning. Mankind

- or something similar - is essential to add self-awareness to a Nature which otherwise would be mentally blind. Mankind is matter spiritualised. All matter is potentially spiritual, presumably including stones and flowers.

Kubla Khan illustrates the theory, I think, even though the poem was composed long before he'd formulated it. Coleridge wrote *Kubla Khan*, or so the story goes, in 1797 in a farm house between Linton and Porlock in north Devon. He was reading about the 14th century Kubla Khan, grandson of Genghis, the first non-Han Emperor of China. (The book, *Purchas, His Pilgrimes*, was published in 1613.) Coleridge, high on opium to ease the pain of dysentery, fell asleep and woke to find a whole poem had composed itself in his mind. He was writing it down when, famously, a "Person from Porlock" knocked on the door and the poet (or amanuensis) forgot the ending. God created a wilderness in Mongolia: a man, Kubla Khan, using the same divine but watered-down creativity, turned it into a garden: but then divine Imagination by-passed the poet's consciousness to create a greater garden in the mind of Coleridge, complete with undertones of eternity. The poet is the greater and so …

> … all should cry, Beware! Beware!
> His flashing eyes, his floating hair!
> Weave a circle round him thrice,
> And close your eyes with holy dread,
> For he on honey-dew hath fed,
> And drank the milk of Paradise.

Sir Alister Clavering Hardy, born in Nottingham in 1896, had mystical experiences as a schoolboy in Oundle although he kept them to himself throughout his working life.

He was a zoologist and marine biologist, successively a professor of zoology at the universities of Hull, Aberdeen and

Oxford. In his late thirties he sailed in the Royal Research Ship *Discovery* (Scott's and Shackleton's originally) to study whales in the South Seas. On the voyage, between 1925 and 1927, he invented a device for collecting and preserving unbroken streams of plankton. The Plymouth-based *Sir Alister Hardy Foundation for Ocean Science*, the first of his legacies, has carried on doing so continuously since 1931. In 1940, he was made a Fellow of the Royal Society. In 1957, he was knighted. In the Great War he'd been a Captain in the Northern Cyclist Battalion, a home defence unit which never went to France. He was at Exeter College, Oxford, when war broke out. On top of all that, Hardy was a good amateur watercolourist. Some of his paintings are, of course, of sea life but others are of the island of South Georgia, the Cotswolds, and a series of temples and sacred places in Japan, China and Burma. They are, I think, full of mystical sensitivity, the South Georgia landscapes in particular. Books of some of his paintings have been printed: the University of Wales has the main collection. His last book, *Darwin and the Spirit of Man*, was published in 1984 when he was eighty-eight. He died the following year.

Alan Watts (1915-1973), born in Kent, went to what is perhaps the world's oldest school - The King's (founded 597) in Canterbury - but was influenced by Eastern ideas from the start: at sixteen he was treasurer of the London Buddhist Lodge run by Christmas Humphreys, a barrister. He left for the USA in 1938 (avoiding war service) and studied Zen in New York before becoming an Anglican priest for five years (1945-1950). From 1951 to '57 he taught at the American Academy of Asian Studies in San Francisco. During the '50s, too, he gave weekly talks on the Pacifica Radio station in Berkeley. His voice was rich and he spoke fluently without stumbling, or ever losing his accent (Home Counties Received Pronunciation - Oxford or the Queen's English). In the late 1950s he also had a weekly TV programme in San Francisco: *Eastern Wisdom and Modern Life*. Some of his talks still have millions of visits on Youtube.

He lived, alternatively, in a boat in Sausalito and a cabin on Mount Tamalpais, both in Marin County, California. He had three wives, seven children, and died of drink (or a heart attack).

Aldous Huxley (1894-1963) was of the Great War generation but he didn't serve because of poor sight: for a time he was nearly blind with inflammation of the corneas. During the Great War, he worked as a farm labourer at Garsington, the Oxfordshire retreat of Ottoline Morrell and the Bloomsbury set. Huxley satirised them in his early Post-War novel, *Crome Yellow*. All the same, he met his first wife there, a Belgian woman. Post-War they lived in Italy (close to D H Lawrence) and it was there, in his late thirties, that he wrote *Brave New World*, a novel about a dystopia where children are bred in vats, allotted IQ slots from before birth and drugged into docility throughout their lives with unrefusable sex and a narcotic called *soma* - a Sanskrit word for a real hallucinogen, not the Greek for body. His novel, *Those Barren Leaves* (1925), set in an Italian palace in the little town of Vezza, is about the shallowness, emptiness, sadness, hollowness and alienation of an English cultural elite deprived of the spiritual. The title is from a poem by Wordsworth: the leaves are the pages of books about science which cut us off from truly experiencing the nature of things, which curiously Huxley never did.

In *Ends and Means* (1937) Huxley explains his atheism: "I took it for granted that there was no meaning ... I had motives for not wanting the world to have a meaning; consequently assumed that it had none, and was able without any difficulty to find satisfying reasons for this assumption. ... Those who detect no meaning in the world generally do so because, for one reason or another, it suits their books that the world should be meaningless."

In 1937 he moved to California with his family. The Americans denied him citizenship because he wouldn't swear he'd take up arms in the country's defence: he was a philosophical, not a religious, pacifist. In California he made friends with

212

Kristnamurti and became involved with Vedanta. (It was through Huxley that his fellow Englishman, Christopher Isherwood, became a disciple of Swami Prabhavananda. Huxley wrote the preface to Isherwood's translation of *The Bhagavad Gita*.) He tried his hand at Hollywood movie scripts but was not good at popular stuff: his brother called him an overview man, a universalist (or generalist). Even his novels are about ideas. In temperament and physique he matched the cerebrotonic/ectomorph of William Sheldon's somatotypes. (Huxley knew Sheldon, too.) He died, aged sixty-nine, of throat cancer, within two hours of President Kennedy's assassination and on the same day that C S Lewis died.

Arthur Schopenhauer (1788-1860) was the victim of his own dictum. He was a mystic, a materialist and an atheist who saw, not eternity, but only a material universe, a place of unmitigated misery, cruelty and barbarity. Only two things made it bearable - art and the moment of mystical awareness. What Kant had called the noumenon, Schopenhauer seems to have thought of as pure energy - perhaps like Heraclitean Fire - which evolved locally into matter, plants, life and mind but is itself mindless and driven by its own mindless nature.

In the 1730s, **George Berkeley** (1685-1753), already an immaterialist but not yet a Bishop, was living on a farm in Rhode Island waiting for the Government back home to help him set up a college in Bermuda to train missionaries to work in the American colonies. While there, he wrote *Alciphron*, a defence of Christianity against freethinking atheists whose aim was to tear down capitalism and change society. The political and religious system was already being brought slowly down, says Alciphron. Prejudice against atheism "lessens every day among the better sort; and when it is quite worn out, our Free-thinkers may then (and not till then) be said to have given the finishing Stroke to Religion." Once the root is gone, the shoots will perish too and with them "Notions of Conscience, Duty, Principle, and the like, which fill a Man's Head with Scruples, awe him with Fears, and make him a more thorough Slave than the Horse he rides".

The astonished Euphranor, a Christian, tells Alciphron that the Gentlemen of his Sect are "admirable Weeders" but what will they grow in their place? The "Appetites, Passions and Senses", says Alciphron, echoing the Sophists of Socratic Athens. "Food, Drink, Sleep, and the like animal Enjoyments being what all Men like and love."

The future Bishop also foresaw the way the fall of the West could be brought about. To begin with by taking over the meaning of words and corrupting the language. Control language and you control what people can think. The Free-thinkers were already changing the world by re-naming the vices - a crook is "a Man who knows the Ways of the World", a card sharp is a "Man who plays the Game", "a vicious Man" (a man, that is, given over to vice) "is a Man of Pleasure".

Berkeley even foresaw the "long march through the institutions". Lysicles, the Atheist Free-thinker, says that members of his Sect have been secretly infiltrating society for years - "working like Moles under Ground, concealing our Progress from the Public". Soon the ideas of his Sect will sprout unaided, untended, in minds which have been already ploughed, planted and weeded. People won't even know what's been done to them as they accept previously alien ideas as their own. But why be secretive? "A Rebellion, or an Invasion, alarms and puts the Public upon its Defence; but a Corruption of Principles works its Ruin more slowly perhaps, but more surely."

In other words destroy the spiritual, corrupt the language, colonise the minds of a deprived and emptied society.

Immaterialism. Erigena in the 9th century may have been the first Western immaterialist, followed eight centuries later by Malebranche and then by Arthur Collier, a Wiltshire vicar, and his Irish contemporary, Bishop Berkeley. The vicar is now forgotten: the Bishop is *the* immaterialist. (Plotinus, I suppose, was an immaterialist without knowing it). Berkeley, a Christian

Platonist like Erigena, thought the physical world is a thought in God's mind. Everything is held in a mind - or Mind - and there's no evidence of anything outside it: after all, you can't climb out to check.

Immaterialism then seems to have died until the late 19th century when at least two recruits appeared. A A Luce (1882-1977), Berkeley's biographer and a Professor of philosophy in Trinity College, Dublin, became an immaterialist after studying the old Bishop. He was also the first, I think, to point out that Berkeley owed a lot to Nicholas Malebranche (1638- 1715). Malebranche played with the idea that the things of the world are nothing more than ideas in God's mind, but retreated into dogma (he was a monk in Paris) for comfort and safety.

In his book, *Sense without Matter* (1956), Luce writes: "Descartes and Malebranche have weighed matter in the balance of reason and found it wanting. They have tried to fit it into their theories of perception and have failed. Does matter exist? They asked the question and burked the answer." Luce, from Gloucestershire, was awarded the Military Cross as an officer in the Royal Irish Rifles in the Great War (he'd been a student at Trinity College, Dublin). He was also a chess-playing fly fisherman whose motto was "fishing and philosophy: trout and truth".

Sir James Jeans (1877-1946) was a physicist and mathematician known for the Jeans Length or Jeans Instability which says that a cloud of interstellar gas with a radius less than the Jeans Length will fly apart, unable to collapse into a new star. "I incline to the idealistic theory that consciousness is fundamental, and that the material universe is derivative from consciousness, not consciousness from the material universe. In general the universe seems to me to be nearer to a great thought than to a great machine."

Oddly enough, Pierre Gassendi (1592-1655), one of the first modern materialists, had something to add: whatever is immaterial must be immortal.

This idea of a **mind-made world** was not entirely original. Xenophanes of Colophon (c570-c475 BC) also thought we make the world we live in our own heads and we can therefore never get at the whole truth. "The cosmos is a web of guesses". He also added the famous idea that if cows had gods, and could draw, then their gods would look like cows. Xenophanes is also sometimes called the first Western monotheist, though henotheist is probably better - he believed in a supreme God among many lesser ones. This God moves all things by power of mind which Xenophanes still imagined to be made of matter. He was a poet, not a philosopher.

Alfred Noyes (1880-1958) was born in Wolverhampton but grew up in Aberystwyth. His father was a grocer who, in an odd career change, switched to teaching Greek and Latin. Noyes himself failed to get a degree because he was in London talking to his poetry publisher instead of taking his finals in Oxford. Six years later he married the daughter of a colonel who'd served in the US Civil War. At thirty-four he was appointed visiting professor of modern English literature in Princeton. As a poor sighted pacifist he spent the second half of the Great War working with John Buchan on propaganda. He was forty-seven when his first wife died and he married his second, a Catholic (to which religion he converted). They lived on the Isle of Wight.

Noyes is almost completely forgotten now and even in the 1950s, when he was an old man but still alive, he was best - perhaps only - known for a single poem: *The Highwayman*:

The wind was a torrent of darkness among the gusty trees.
The moon was a ghostly galleon tossed upon cloudy seas.
The road was a ribbon of moonlight over the purple moor,
And the highwayman came riding -
Riding - riding -
The highwayman came riding, up to the old inn-door.

Bess the inn-keeper's black-eyed daughter kills herself with a musket, hoping the noise of the shot will warn her returning lover that the Redcoats are lying in wait. Tim, the mad-eyed ostler with "hair like mouldy hay", has betrayed him. Next day, when he hears what happened, the highwayman gallops back to the inn and is killed like a dog in the dust. Noyes wrote the poem, set on Bagshot Heath in Surrey, in two days in 1906.

In 1942 Noyes published *The Edge of the Abyss*, a series of lectures he'd given in Canada. His theme was the future of the West under collectivist, statist, totalitarian regimes and the consequential decay of morals and even common decency. His answer was a return to Christianity. In a review of the book Orwell agreed with the diagnosis but not the remedy: Christianity was lost to Europe forever.

Noyes was right in thinking the would-be destroyers "usually have a grudge against civilisation, and nearly always an intense hatred of their own country." But he was wrong in saying "the destructive mind can only exist when it is in a very small minority. As soon as it is the majority the civilisation by which it is produced comes to an end." Even as he writing this in 1921 Antonio Gramsci in distant Italy was working out that the majority neither matters nor counts when a suitably colonised minority runs a country from the top - an infected professoriate is all you need to bring a place to ruin.

Stéphane Mallarmé, the French Symbolist poet, may also have thought that Beauty and the Ultimate (not God) were the same thing - not God because Mallarmé was an atheist, opposed to both religion and science since neither led to the truth. His symbols were designed to by-pass what Robert Graves called "prose meaning" and deliver you straight to the mystic meeting point. Baudelaire had a similar idea: the artist's job is to "clarify and express the consciousness which acts within the material world, but at the same time transcends time and space".

Bruno Snell (1896-1986) was a German philologist who began his career reading economics and law in both Edinburgh and Oxford. Later he held the chair of philology in Hamburg University. Among other things he founded the *Europa-Kolleg Hamburg* where post-graduates study European integration.

G K Chesterton (1874-1936) was a mystic, although an unlikely one - a twenty stone journalist (novelist, detective story writer, radio broadcaster, poet) with a sword stick and cloak. All the same he had at least one mystical experience, in 1894, when he was at the Slade School of Art. Mysticism he thought was merely common sense although it changed his life. He described it in a poem, *The Beatific Vision*:

> O light uplifted from all mortal knowing,
> Send back a little of that glimpse of thee.
> That of its glory I may kindle glowing
> One tiny spark for all men yet to be.

He wrote millions of words - eighty books alone and even, for eleven years, his own magazine, *G K's Weekly* - too much for the undedicated to read but probably in there somewhere is something for all. In *Orthodoxy* (1908) he tells us that the Transcendent is like the sun - a "blaze and a blur": reason is like the moon - a cold Euclidean circle: by relying too much on reason, reason has reasoned itself into near extinction. "The poet only asks to get his head in the heavens. It is the logician who seeks to get the heavens into his head. And it is his head that splits." In *The Defendant* (1901), he also says: "The simple sense of wonder at the shape of things is the basis of spirituality" but the logical and over-rational can't see it. That is one of way of describing Platonism but Chesterton can best be called a Christian Aristotelian or Thomist (or Catholic).

As a Thomist, Chesterton missed out on the Platonist's conception of eternity and had to resort to proofs. In *The Everlasting Man* (1925) he argues that if the human is just another animal, it's a uniquely odd one. Likewise, if Christ was just another preacher/leader he, too, was uniquely odd, as is the Church.

Chesterton became a Christian in 1896 but not a Catholic until 1922. He was also a Distributist - the Catholic middle way between Capitalism and Socialism. To put it very crudely - Capitalism (a few individuals own all), Socialism (individuals own nothing), Distributism (all own all).

Two stories are commonly told about him. He was very absent minded and relied on his wife, Frances (née Blogg). Once he sent her a telegram: "Am in Market Harborough. Where ought I to be?" Wife's reply: "Home."

He's often also quoted as saying: "When men cease to believe in God, they do not then believe in nothing, they believe in anything". The American Chesterton Society think they've traced its origin to a Father Brown short story, *The Oracle of the Dog*: "The first effect of not believing in God is to believe in anything."

Index

A

Adams, Ansel 79-80
alliterative poetry 70
The Am (see also *The Is*) 26, 154
Anaximander 199
Ancients, The 84
Architecture expresses spirit of
 the age 98, 105; Gothic 42, 97;
 Renaissance 97-98; Ruskin's
 advice 204; Ruskin the critic 96
Aristotelianism 20, 26, 198, 218
Arnold, Matthew ix; best self 15,
 cultural Platonism (Hellenism)
 13-16, 173, 177; *Culture and
 Anarchy* 13; *Dover Beach* 15,
 123; poetry as religion 164;
 Empedocles on Etna 70, 196-
 199; Hebraism 14, 189; not a
 mystic 189, 196; the Philistines
 118-119; poetry as religion 14;
 problems with the English 14,
 The Scholar Gipsy 55-61, 90,
 168; Sophocles 15; self actuali-
 sation 15; "sweetness and light"
 14, 118, 137, 142; summary
 176, 177
Arnold, Thomas 46, 137
Arts, the purpose 4, 89, 164; connect to eternity 176; decline
 163-168; mirrors society 176;
 Mystical in Art/Life/Nature
 42; spiritualised by beauty 42

B

Bacon, Francis (Lord Verulam) 51,
 192-194, 208
Ballad of the White Horse, The
 170-171
Barzun, Jacques 66, 81, 194, 195
Bashō, Matsuo 74
beauty *passim*; aim of education
 42; by-passing beauty 125-126;
 connects to eternity x, 3-4, 7,
 9, 26, 42, 68, 76, 97, 98, 101,
 102, 103, 104, 109, 159, 165,
 176, 177, 186, 217; Goodness
 & Truth 175-176; makes us
 bigger and better 189; matches
 rightness of reality 68; music
 89, 92; painting 97; poetry
 67, 68, 69-70, 76, 125-126,
 167; Spirit behind beauty 42;
 spiritual in own right 42; and
 Truth 42
Being/Becoming 63, 65, 72
belonging, see cohesive society
Benson, A C 43-47, 50, 51, 52,
 54

Berkeley, George (Bishop) 154,
    155, 177, 213-214, 215
Betjeman, John 10
Beyond, The x, 76, 79, 80, 85, 89,
    104
bird song 89
Blake, William 83, 84, 85, 145,
    164, 199
Bloom, Harold 64-65, 194
Blyth, R H 9,74, 187-188
Botticelli 80
Bridges, Robert 60-61
Burke, Edmund 79, 115, 142
Burton, Robert 86

C

Cambridge Platonists 153
Camus, Albert 160
Carlyle, Thomas 45, 46, 48, 89, 96,
    102, 105, 139
Carpenter, Edward 80
Chesterton, G K 50, 60, 170-171,
    177, 218-219
Christianity (see also Origen and
    Eckhart) 5, 17-20; Anglican
    128; Aristotelian 195, 218;
    de-Platonised 20; deals with
    pain better 129, 130; defence of
    213; ebbing 123, 143, 148, 159,
    164, 214, 217; emotion-driven
    189; essence 40, 189; essential
    for culture 17; last creative act
    of Antiquity 17; institution-
    alised 19-20; mystery religion
    18-19; St Paul's evolution
    18-19; Protestant Bible religion
    191; religion of the spirit 18;
    Reformation 20; regeneration

from within 96; and reason
    154; values 17, 40-41
Christian Platonism 5, 26, 27,
    39-42, 107, 149, 214
Civil War 46
Clerisy, the 16, 142, 176
Clifford, William Kingdon 22-23
Cohesive societies 8, 98, 105,164,
    202
Coleridge, S T biography 139, 207-
    208; Carlyle's summary 139;
    cast of mimd 119; clerisy 16,
    142, 176; abstract concept of
    Christianity 140-141; esemplas-
    tic power 119; brought Idealism
    140, 141; divides mankind 192;
    God within us 141; general
    influence 140; in Germany
    121, 208; hunger for eternity
    140; illuminated mind 142;
    imagination/reason 141-142;
    on Kant 156; the Logos within
    140-141; in Malta 140, 208; his
    philosophy 140-142; matter is
    potentially conscious 141, 210;
    mystical experience 140; per-
    soneity 140; on the picturesque
    204; introduced new poetry 119;
    Romanticism 119; Schelling
    140, 141; in Scotland 127,
    129, 204; the sublime 205; in
    Westmorland 127, 128; helped
    Wordsworth 118-119, 121-122,
    133; splits with Wordsworth
    208; in summary 176, 177
Collier, Arthur 214
Consciousness altered by drugs
    145; cosmic 21; expanded 4,
    64, 189, 157; and eternity 26,

80, 146, 186, 189, 217; God as higher 26, 72; imagination 210; Imagism 167; immaterialist 155, 215; oddity of 144, 157, 177; Nietzsche 158; self-consciousness, a hindrance 189; social consciousness 207

Cotman, John Sell 45, 83

Crabbe, George 45-46, 53, 133

Critical Thinking 23

Cult of beauty 42

Cultural Marxism 154, 159, 160, 177

D

Dali, Salvador 165

Darbishire, Helen 32, 35, 113, 118, 122, 192

Darwin, Charles 93, 107, 121, 196, 211

Decline of the West 143-144, 148, 153-161, 194

Dialectical Materialism 157

Distributism 219

Duchamp, Marcel 165

E

Eckhart, Meister 26, 145

Eleusinian Mysteries 19, 190

Edward Elgar 92-93

Education debt to Antiquity 13; Newman 15; Oxford 114-115; Ruskin reforms 101; Caroline Spurgeon 191, 192; self-education ix; Wilde/Plato 42

Eliot, T S 7, 101, 188; dying fall 94; Julian of Norwich 185-186; *Notes Towards a Definition of Culture* 16; meaning in poetry 77; old man in a dry month 5; not a mystic 168; results of loss of Christianity 17; Tiresias 154; *The Wasteland* 167-168, 196; summary 176

empiricism 140, 154, 186

emptiness (see the void)

English 71

Enigma Variations 92-93

Enlightenment, the 154, 155

Erigena 214-215

eschatology 18, 25-28

eternity *passim*; see beauty; see soul

Evans, Sir Arthur 60

Existentialism 154, 159, 160

expanded mind 13-16

Expressionism 82, 165

extrovertive mysticism 7, 81, 115, 150, 186

F

Faith all you need 20; faith in place of proof 23-24; lovers of nature 104; common faith for sense of belonging 98, 105; Kant 156; loss of faith 14, 105, 107; choose to have faith 123; through childish need for God's protection 131

Ficino, Marsilio 80, 81

Fitzgerald, Edward 11, 43-54

folk music 202-203

Fors Clavigera 100, 204,

Fox, Adam 4, 183, 185

fragments (see also undertones) 7, 8, 9, 10, 43, 55, 69

Frankfurt School, The 159, 161
French New Left 154
Freud, Sigmund 22

G

Gassendi, Pierre 177, 215
Gauguin, Paul 82,
Gilpin, William ("Picturesque")
    103, 128, 204, 205
Greensleeves 90
God 18, 19, 22, 23-24, 26, 34, 35,
    104; eternity and God 123;
    faith in protection 131; what
    does the word mean? 25
Godhead 26, 180
gods, the 14, 20, 36, 40, 44, 74, 75,
    83, 105, 119, 170, 197, 198,
    216,
Godwinism 116, 134, 196
golden melancholy 86
Goldsmith, Oliver 10
Gothic architecture 42, 97, 106,
    158, 205
Gramsci, Antonio 159, 177, 217
Gray, Thomas 10
groupthink 166-167

H

haiku 74-75, 167
Hardy, Sir Alister 143-145, 177,
    210-211
Hawkes, Jacquetta 10
Hebraism 14, 189
Hegel, G W F 156-157, 186
Heidegger, Martin 159-160
Hellenism 14, 189
Hinduism 80

Ho Estin (see also *The Is*) 26
Hopkins, G M 184
Horkheimer, Max 161, 177
Housman, A E 73-74, 201-202
Holman Hunt, Willliam 106
Hume, David 23, 115, 176
Hutchinson, Mary 114, 117, 127
Hutchinson, Sara 208
Huxley, Aldous 147-148, 177,
    212-213

I

Ibsen, Henrik 65-66, 194
Idealism 140, 141, 151, 157, 208
Illumination x, 4, 8, 15, 55, 69, 71,
    142, 153, 176
immaterialism 5, 24, 26, 89, 97, 109,
    153, 155, 175, 176, 177, 213-215
Impressionism 81-82, 107
Incompletes 18-19, 156
Idealism 140, 141, 154, 15, 208
Industrialism 95, 98, 169
Inge, W R biography 183-184;
    peak art? 163-164; Cambridge
    Platonists 153; *Christian
    Mysticism* 149; Christian
    Platonism 39; don't ask does
    God exist 176; end of great art?
    163, 176; immaterial eternal
    values 175-176; forgetting the
    past 169, 175; fragility of the
    West 175; make your own reli-
    gion 3, 175; mysticism - what
    it isn't 187; Paul Nash 83; real
    newness 167; 19th century
    greatest of them all 175; on
    Platonism 3, 103, 183, 184,
    185; Platonism basis of his

belief 184; on poetry 67, 163; questionnaires 143; regeneration from within 96; religion based on experience of the unseen (which he didn't have) 183; religion comes from within 21, 175; rage against the Victorians 167; reviews Noyes - group-think 166-167; on Ruskin 108; swamp when religious life lost 3; on the two worlds 3, 67, 163, 175; on Wordsworth 31; summary 175-176

introvertive mysticism 7, 81, 150, 186

Is, The (see also *The Am*) 18, 26, 154

Islands of the Blest 69

J

James, William without the divine 23, 191; good outcomes 25; lyrical enchantment 177, 191; science 143

Japanese understanding of sadness 9

Jeans, James 215

Julian of Norwich 185

K

Kant, Immanuel 141, 154, 155-156, 159, 213

Kubla Khan 210

L

lacrimae rerum see sadness and repose

Lamb, Charles 140

Lark Ascending, The 89, 90-91

Laski, Marghanita 147-151

last things see eschatology

Leith Hill 87, 200, 202

Leuba, James Henry 143

Locke, John 121, 142

Luce, A A 215

Luther, Martin 20, 65

M

Malebranche 214

Mallarmé, Stéphane 82, 167, 217

materialism Berkeley 177; West's default position 24, 143-144, 154; Dialectical 157; Empedocles 196; Freud 22; Gassendi 215; Hobbes 153; Locke142; Ruskin 99; Schopenhauer 213; university studies 16; the Welfare State 102

Marx, Karl 157, 159

Marxism 154, 157, 159, 160, 177

Marcuse, Herbert 160

Masefield, John 8, 9, 55, 60, 68-70, 71, 77, 187

melody 68, 89-90, 92

Meredith, George 90-91

Middle Ages 97, 105, 151

Mill, J S 99, 140

Milton, John 54, 86, 132, 195, 200

Minor Third 93-94

Modernism 83, 163-168; modified by mysticism 83-84

moonlight in art 71-72, 84

Monet, Claude 80-82, 107

More, Thomas 101

Morris, William 99

Munch, Edvard 66, 82, 165

Music beauty the source of harmony
92; melody 68, 89-90, 92; harmonises the soul 92; minor third
92, 94; and mysticism 89; Plato
- makes people complete, loud
music destroys 92; what makes it
work? 89, 91, 92; and Platonism
79; Plotinus - order and beauty
92; Pythagoras and cosmic order
91-92; single note can connect
92; universal rules 97

Mysticism (same as Platonism)
Matthew Arnold 189, 196;
Catholicism 19; GK Chesterton
218; definitions x, 4, 26, 36,
97, 144, 186, 191; different
consciousness 186; cosmic consciousness 21; drugs 147-149;
an experience 21; extrovertive
7, 115; Far Eastern 145-146;
how it works - blocked thought
7, 18, 36, 186, 189, 190, 196,
198, 204-205; RW Inge 184;
hesychasm 147, 190-191;
introvertive 7, 146, 148; Laski
149-151; Mystical in Art/Life/
Nature 42 painting 82-83; Plato
4, 146; poetry and place 10; *The
Prelude* 129; Roland Romain 22;
salvation via 68-69, 186; science
21, 143-145; Caroline Spurgeon
191-192; WT Stace 186-187;
what is it? 36-37; What is it
like? peace 4, 9, 18, 26, 27, 31,
36, 65, 68, 80, 84, 103-104,
109, 144, 146, 150, 181, 186,
192, 198; changelessness 97;

dissolving x; lyrical enchantment 191; pure consciousness
26; touches nature of Being 28;
sense of oneness 31, 97, 146,
168, 191, 192; who? 21, 144-
145, 149-150, 209; Wilde 42;
summary 176

N

Nash, Paul 82-84

Neo-Marxism 154, 177

Newman, John 15-16, 142, 176

Nietzsche, Friedrich 157-159, 176

Noyes, Alfred 165-167, 176,
216-217

O

Olympic games 101

Origen 26-27, 146

Orphism 19

P

Paglia, Camille 157

painting Platonist painting 79-87;
Platonist painting's antithesis
82; the Renaissance 80; Ruskin
on 96-97, 104-105; typological
106; universal rules 97; Wilde
on modern painting 81

Palmer, Samuel 83, 84-87,
199-200

Paul, St 17-19, 20, 186

Personeity 140-141

Phenomenology 159-160

photography 79-80

Picasso, Pablo 82, 83, 163

Picturesque, the 103, 114, 204

Plato *passim* and Orphism 19; Freud 24; education 42; eternity 26; and Popper 193; Renaissance - mysticism without Plato 143-151; 80

Platonism *passim* (see also beauty, music, mysticism, plays, poetry, Welfare State) critical thinking 21; defined 3-5, 13, 18, 177, 191; and beauty 42; Robert Bridges versifies Plato; 60-61; based on an experience which can end 125-126; a living faith 3, 103; can't be falsified 23-24; immaterialist 26; Platonism lost 22, 143-151; message 13; a monist philosophy 23-24; as mysticism 4; has to be self-taught ix; way of the intellect 4, 13-16

Poetry (see also undertones) beauty in despair 76; beauty in elemental forces 76; brevity needed 74-75; based on languages's deepest characteristic 70; form and content 69-70; should lodge fragments in the mind 9, 69; harmonises the soul 92; 67-68; to harmonise the sadness of the universe 68; of ideas 70, 195-196; need the invisible to create it 105, 166; of ideas 195-196; the language of eternity 67; Middle English poetry 70-71; moonlight 71-72; Old English poetry 70; great poetry implicit in Platonism 163; power of lesser poets 69; poetry as religion 14, 164; importance of meaning 77-78; Platonism of poetry and place 55; poetry in people 76; poetry in the sound of words 72, 73, 77-78; how poetry works Platonically 67, 68, 72-73; sadness and repose 34-35; as search for truth 67; as the way of beauty 4, 72-73; rhyme 71; sadness in poetry 73-74; universal rules 97

Plotinus 21, 78, 80, 92, 144, 145, 184, 214

Popper, Karl 193

Post-Modernism 66, 153-161

Pound, Ezra 167

Pre-Raphaelite Brotherhood 106-107

Pythagoras 19, 91-92

Q

Quantock Hills 8, 84, 117, 119

R

Rationalism 150, 153, 154

Religion *passim* from within 175-175; of the Spirit 18, 20, 186

Renaissance, The 20, 42, 80, 97, 106, 130

rhyme 67

Rolland, Romain 22, 192

Romanticism 81, 119, 140, 209

Rousseau, Jean-Jacques 154, 156

Ruskin, John *passim Aesthetics/ theoria* 103; "age of umber" 105; anti-capitalist 99; art critic 96-97; on

architecture 42, 96, 97-98,
105, 204; art is praise 67; art
as touchstone 105; as an artist
96-97, 107; beauty and eternity
103, 109; beauty and the divine
98; "bigger and better" 16, 42,
109, 189;Christianity 107-108;
loss of faith 107-108; *Fors
Clavigera* 100-101, 204; great
art and cohesion 105; great man
theory 102; Guild of St George
100; Housman on 201-202;
immaterial more important
than matter 176; Industrial
Revolution 98; loss of faith 107-
108; people he influenced 101;
isolates "sadness and repose" 9,
35-36, 105; Law of Cooperation
98; Law of Help 97, 201;
mystical experiences 103-104
- art induces then 104, 105;
mountainous landscape induces
them 104; National Trust 100;
Platonism not enough 108-
109; a Platonist 96, 107; PRB
106-107; Rose la Touche 108;
and the *Rubaiyat* 49; self-actu-
alisation 98-99; social reform
109; on Turner 96-97, 104-105;
typological painting 106-107;
identifies ugliness as destructive 98; Welfare State 95-102;
Whistler 107

S

Sabatier, Auguste 18
sadness and repose in great art
105; exiled from home 68;
mystical experience 209; fleetingness of things 11, 75, 176;
at the heart of life 90; sadness
of loneliness of things 9; Minor
Third 93-94; for our mortality
80, 93; Ruskin isolates feeling 9; sadness of things 54,
68, 73, 85-86; in sunlight 84;
and undertones 4, 9, 92, 180;
sadness in words 77-78; in
Wordsworth 35-36
Sartre, Jean-Paul 160
Stace, Walter Terence 150, 186-187
Schelling, F W J von 35, 140, 141,
209-210
Scholar Gipsy, The 55-61, 90, 168
Schopenhauer, Arthur 176, 213
Scruton, Roger 7, 27, 160
Sitwell, Edith 90
Shakespeare, William 45, 63,
64-65, 140, 164, 165, 194Snell,
Bruno 168, 218
Smith, Adam 99
socialism 39, 96, 140, 195, 203-
204, 219
Socrates 144, 146, 157, 158, 159,
173, 194
Sophocles 53, 165; see life steadily
15, 23, 65, 118, 142, 176
Soul senses eternity 5, 26, 28, 177;
what adds to 189; art 166;
beauty and the soul 42, 54,
67-68, 84, 104; celestial light
132; Cross and immortality
27; best self 189; city in the
soul 69; distress and the soul
130; harmonise 158; Origen's
27; Platonist/Aristotelian 20,
192; sense-soul 185; stillness

and the soul 86; tripartite 22; unknowable 42; Wilde on the soul 42; raise above the worldly to sense divinity 146-147

Spengler, Oswald 82

Spinoza 121

Spurgeon, Caroline 21, 31, 148-149, 193

Starbuck, Edwin Diller 143

Stewart, J A 125, 185; definition of Platonism 4, 177

surrealism 82, 165

"sweetness and light" 14, 118, 137, 142

Symbolism 82, 84, 217

T

tears for things see sadness and repose

Thomas, R S 209

Tennyson, Lord Alfred 44, 45, 46, 52, 68, 105, 123, 187, 196

Thomas Tallis Suite 90, 91-91

Thomson, James (BV) 76-77

Tintern Abbey 33, 122

topophilia 10

Towne, Francis 83-84

Transcendent, the 132, 144, 149-150, 154, 157, 164, 172, 196; like the sun 218

Transcendentalism 140

Treasure Island 10

Turner, J M W 96, 104-105, 130, 201

U

Ugliness active and destructive x, 4, 65, 98, 176; disconnects from eternity 65; disobey rules of music 92; of ego 18, 72; of emptiness 28; etymology 71; industrial 98, 135; of modern towns 95; symptom of disease in society163; Plato's philosopher-kings raised without it 92; Ruskin first to see its destructiveness 98

Undertones (see also fragments) ix, 7-11, 207; art should generate 4, 63-64; in children's books 10-11; daily miracle 4, 199; defined 4, 7-8; Dorothy Wordsworth 118; Japanese deeper insight 9, 74; in landscape 56; in life stories 11, 43, 53; in moonlight 71-72; in music 92; in poetry 55, 69, 132, 210; reminders of eternity 108, 176; sadness and repose 4, 9; in deep time 10

Symbolism 84

Utopia. 101, 151, 160, 208

W

Watts, Alan 146, 211-212

Way of the Intellect 119

Way of Beauty (see also "sweetness and light") 67-68, 186, 119

Welfare State (see also Ruskin) 95, 96, 99, 101-102

Whistler, James 107

Whitman, Walt 80

Whittenham Clumps 83

Wilde, Oscar 27, 39-42, 63, 81, 100, 203-204

Williams, Ralph Vaughan 87, 89-91, 177, 200-201, 202-203

Wordsworth, Dorothy 8, 117, 118, 127-129, 204, 205-207

Wordsworth, William (see also Coleridge and Dorothy)
Platonist trajectory - childhood/early manhood experiences 7, 32-35; vocation 115; lost his way 114-116; Coleridge's influence on 118-119, 121, 133, 135; Dorothy's influence on 118-119; great decade 32-33, 84; Romanticism 119; social reform 115, 119-120; reforms poetry 33, 119; loss of Platonist insight 125-126, 132, 133; Platonism not enough - death of brother 129; Christianity 122-123; how Christian? 132-133; early life 114; pre-marriage Grasmere 127-129; later family life 126, 134, 136-137.
Platonist poems: *Intimations of Immortality* 33, 38, 69, 122, 126; *The Prelude* (Books I, II, XIII) 32, 33, 35, 113, 114, 116, 118, 121, 122-123, 129; *Tintern Abbey* 33, 34, 122. Industrialism 135; General Election136; rejects cult of the picturesque 204; poet laureate187; politics 116, 134-135; opposed Lakeland railway 135; and Ruskin 108-109; sadness and repose 35-36; stamp collector 135-136; tourism 115, 134, 204-206

V

Void, the spiritual x, 7, 27-28, 65, 146, 157, 160, 164, 176, 188, 195, 196, 212

X

Xenophanes of Colophon 195, 216

Y

Yeats, W B 70, 78, 104, 153, 188

Z

Zen 74, 80, 146, 160, 211